# The Mastery Of Self And The Mastery Of Fate

## Christian D. Larson

ISBN 1425482449

# Mastery of Self

BY

## CHRISTIAN D. LARSON

*Editor of*

ETERNAL PROGRESS

AND

THE COSMIC WORLD

L. N FOWLER & CO.
7, Imperial Arcade, Ludgate Circus
LONDON, E. C.

1908
THE PROGRESS COMPANY
CHICAGO

# Mastery of Self

**M**AN is made for attainment and achievement; to ever become greater and greater than he is now—that is the purpose of his life; and to promote that purpose he must ever advance in the mastery of self. To move forward in the path of attainment, everything in the being of man must be employed constructively; every process in mind or body must become a building process, and all the elements and forces in the human system must work together towards the great goal in view; but to direct the whole of self to work for a greater self demands the mastery of self.

No power in man can do what it is created to do, and what it has the capacity to do, until it is directed by man himself; powers, elements, forces and things are at the disposal of man; they can do only what he directs them to do; they respond only to his control, but before man can gain the power to master forces and things, he must gain the power to master himself.

When man has gained the power to control himself he can control everything in his world without trying to control anything. It is therefore evident that he who is trying to control everything has not learned how to control anything. The true master never tries to master anything, not even himself. He does not have to try to be a master—he is a master.

Nor is it necessary to try to be a master in order to reach that state where one is a master; in fact no person can learn to control himself so long as he tries to control himself.

To eliminate every desire to master oneself is the first step towards the attainment of the mastery of self. He who does not wish to control anything is alone prepared to gain the power to control everything.

He who tries to control himself, or who tries to control anything that exists outside of himself gives everything in his being the tendency to work towards the surface; the power that produces the mastery of self, however, can only be gained by training the mind to move in the opposite direction.

To master self is to have the power to produce any effect desired in any part of mind or body, and to produce any effect desired it is necessary to produce the corresponding cause; but to produce any cause the mind must act in the world of cause—a world which exists, not on the surface of thought or being, but in the great within.

The harder one tries to control himself the nearer to the surface will the mind act, and the further will mental action be separated from that interior mental state from which one may gain the power to control himself.

He who tries to attain the mastery of self will act entirely upon the outer mental world of effect, and will therefore be unable to create the cause that can produce the mastery of self. The mind must act back of, beneath and above the effect in order to change or produce the cause.

The state of self-mastery is an effect; it is the result of certain attainments; therefore, to produce the state of self-mastery, one must not act upon the state of self-mastery, but must proceed to promote those attainments that naturally result in self-mastery.

It is not possible, however, to promote these attainments while the mind is trying to exercise control over things; to try to control things is to think about things and act directly upon things, and no mind that is acting upon things can act upon the power that controls things.

Each power in the being of man will, when expressed, do the very thing that it is naturally adapted for; that is, it will produce its own natural effect; therefore, to secure any desired effect, the secret is to awaken that power that will, of itself, produce that effect.

However, to awaken any power in the being of man, the mind must act directly upon that state where the power originates; and every power in man originates in the great within.

There is an inner source of everything that appears in the human personality, and to master self is to have the power to cause this inner source to bring forth into the personal self whatever we desire to have expressed through the self.

What the self is to be, and to do, is determined by what is expressed through the self; therefore, when we can cause the inner source to bring forth into the self whatever we may desire, the self will be and do whatever we may desire. And when we can cause the self to be what we wish it to be, and do what we wish it to do, at any time and under any circumstance, then it is that we have gained the mastery of self.

**T**HE mastery of self is an attainment that has no end. Though everything in mind and body may be mastered today, tomorrow will bring forth from the great within new forces, new talents, new powers and new fields of consciousness, all of which demand control and direction if they are to serve their purpose and be of the greatest possible use to man.

Everything that exists in the being of man is created for some purpose, and the whole of life is not lived as it is intended to be lived unless every such purpose is fulfilled; but nothing in man can fulfill its purpose unless it is mastered by the ruling power in man.

The attainment of self-mastery is therefore indispensable to the living of life, and the promotion of the greatest welfare of the whole of life.

Those elements, forces, faculties, talents and functions that are only partially under control do not serve the life of man as extensively as they might; in fact, many of these, even those that we have been conscious of for ages, serve us but little; and the cause is deficiency in the art of self-mastery.

There are only a few minds that accomplish as much with their talents as it is possible to accomplish at present; the majority, even among the most gifted, seldom use their ability in its full capacity because they have only a limited control over that ability.

That person who has perfect control of himself can accomplish from two to five times as much with a given talent as those who have no more self-control than is found among the average.

To those who seek to attain much and achieve much, self-mastery is therefore invaluable, though it is equally important in the minor affairs of every-day life; a fact that will readily be admitted when we realize how much distress comes hourly to millions because they cannot control their feelings, emotions, thoughts and actions.

A large share of the mistakes that are made every moment, can be traced directly to a lack of self-control; and the same can be said of sickness, trouble and failure. To have health, happiness and harmony, peace, power and plenty, self-mastery, to a high degree, is necessary; in brief, the only life that is worth while is the life that is lived in the mastery of self.

To attain the mastery of self, it is first necessary to establish firmly in mind the fundamental purpose of mastery. This is extremely important because to proceed with the wrong purpose in view is to make every effort useless. This, however, is what has been done by nearly everyone who has undertaken the attainment of self-mastery; and nearly all the books that have been written on the subject have been based upon the wrong purpose; they have therefore retarded the very thing which they aimed to promote.

This being true, it is simple to understand why it is practically impossible to find a single person who has attained complete mastery over self.

Nearly every system purporting to teach the art of self-mastery has been based upon the purpose of controlling something, or exercising arbitrary rulership over mind, body, circumstances and things. But so long as the mind is trying to control something, the power that can control that something will not be gained.

We must remember, at the very beginning that before the power of self-mastery can be developed and the state of complete mastery attained, all desire to exercise control over anything or anybody must be eliminated absolutely.

The purpose of self-mastery is to give the mind the power to make the fullest and the most perfect use of all the gifts that one may possess now; to be one's best in every sense of the term, at all times, and under all circumstances; to fulfill the purpose of life thoroughly during every passing moment; to live a larger life, a better life and a more beautiful life every day; to be all that one can be now, and to do all that one can do now; to bring forth continually the very best that may exist in the great within, and to use that best in such a way that the very best will always come to pass.

The true purpose of self-mastery is to make yourself more perfect, more competent and more useful. In other words, to become much and accomplish much, in order that you may not only be your complete self, but also be an inspiration to all those who believe in the new race, the superior race, the race of mental mastery and soul supremacy.

**T**HE problem of causing everything in life to become right
will easily be solved when man
becomes great enough to produce only that which is right;
and this greatness will inevitably come
when the mastery of self is attained.

That man may become infinitely more
than he is now, and that he can do far
greater things than has ever been done
before, we know with a certainty; we also
know that it is the purpose of human life
to go on to greatness and greater greatness,
but every step must be preceded by another
degree in the mastery of self.

When we understand life we invariably
gain a strong desire to develop superiority;
first, because it is right to attain superiority,
and second because we may thereby inspire
thousands to press on to those same mag-
nificent heights.

We desire to demonstrate superiority,
however, not for the sake of applause,
but to prove by example what man can do.
We seek greatness, not that we may rule
over anything or anybody, but that we may
fulfill the law of life which declares that
man is created to become greater and greater
so long as eternity shall continue to be.

Our object is not to control those things that exist about us, but to develop those things that exist within us. We seek the fulness of life, and the power to be of the greatest possible use in life; and we seek self-mastery because through mastery alone can these things be promoted to the very highest degree.

When the true purpose of self-mastery is firmly established in mind, we may proceed to develop the power that does produce self-mastery; but the true purpose must never be ignored, because growth in mastery will awaken new forces, new states of consciousness and new possibilities, and these must all be properly directed.

The higher the power the stronger its force; therefore, the higher we go in the scale of attainment the more important it becomes to properly direct everything.

The misdirection of the higher forces will not only produce all manner of ills, troubles and failures, but will produce mental phenomena that is misleading. The understanding of truth or any phase of truth will thereby become extremely difficult; in fact it will be practically impossible to know the real truth about anything so long as such misdirections prevail.

To avoid absolutely the misdirection of any power, fix attention upon development; seek the mastery of self and everything that exists in yourself because you desire to promote greatness in yourself, and you will continue to remain on the right path.

When every thought is animated with a strong desire for a more perfect body, a larger mind and a more beautiful soul, every effort towards the attainment of self-mastery will become constructive, and only good results can possibly follow.

The less you think about the outer self, and the more you think about the inner self, the better, because it is through the perfect expression of the inner self that you will gain the power to master the outer self.

To clearly, firmly and permanently establish in mind what one desires to master is extremely important; also, what self-control will mean when it is attained, and what will happen to mind and body when the power of mastery is exercised.

There is a current belief among many that to master oneself is to have the power to interfere with natural functions at will; to suspend the action of this or that organ without producing serious results, and to violate natural laws without having to undergo any of the natural consequences. Others believe that mastery consists in the forceful control of anything and everything that may exist in one's system or in one's circumstances; but such conclusions are the very opposites to the truth.

The majority, however, entertain those very ideas concerning self-mastery; and this is one of the principal reasons why their efforts to attain self-mastery cannot possibly succeed.

He who has attained the mastery of self never tries to suspend the action of any organ; he never thinks of interfering with natural functions in any way whatever, nor does he ignore or violate a single natural law. He never tries to control anything or anybody, not even himself. In fact, the desire to control has been eliminated completely from his mind. His object is not to control himself, but to make the best possible use of himself; and to try to exercise control over something is to interfere with the best use of that something.

The greatest use of self comes directly from the greatest mastery of self, but it is not possible to attain the greatest mastery of self unless the greatest use of self is made the one sole purpose in view.

He who has no desire to control anything, but is inspired with a strong, irresistible desire to make the greatest use of everything, has entered the path to the mastery of self. Without trying to control anything, everything will naturally and willingly come under his control, and will do whatsoever he may wish to have done.

TO master oneself means to direct all the elements, forces, functions and faculties in the system for the purpose of promoting their natural activities to the highest degree of perfection.

To master one's desires does not mean to suspend those desires, but to give those desires more life and power than ever before, and then direct them into channels of action where the greatest and best results can be obtained under present circumstances.

When you have a desire to do a certain thing and the force of that desire is at hand in the system ready to act, but present circumstances will not permit the expression of that desire, instead of suspending that desire, thereby wasting the energy that was ready for action, you simply turn the force of that desire into some other channel. In this way, valuable results may be secured from the force of every desire that appears in the system, whether the original impulse of that desire can be carried out or not.

Whenever a desire is crushed or suspended all the energy that was alive in that desire will be wasted; and the same waste takes place when a desire is carried in the system for hours, days or weeks, to wear itself out, so to speak, without having its active power turned into any channel of constructive action.

To feel a desire is simply to feel the presence of energy; a desire conveys to the mind the fact that there is energy in the system ready to do something; and if this energy is not given the opportunity to do something it will be wasted.

Through the attainment of self-mastery all the energy that comes into action in the system can be turned into any channel of constructive expression that may be convenient at the time; in fact, to master a desire does not mean to suspend that desire so that it is not felt any more, but to change the course of the force that is active in that desire, so that something of value may be accomplished now while that force is in working condition.

The master-mind never destroys a single desire; he not even thinks of putting down a single feeling that may arise in the system; when he cannot carry out the original desire, or when he finds that the original desire is not normal, which is frequently the case, he redirects the forces that are felt in the system causing them to do something else, something that is normal, and that is possible now.

To master the natural functions is not to interfere with the purpose of those functions, but to promote that purpose to the very highest degree of perfection.

You can master a natural function when you can cause that function to perform its work perfectly under all sorts of conditions, and thereafter, to continue to further perfect the perfection of its perfect work.

To master the organs and functions of digestion does not mean that you can cause those organs to digest anything that you might take into the system; self-mastery does not violate law, neither does it willfully admit an enemy in order that it may demonstrate its power to overcome that enemy. Self-mastery does not resist what is not wanted, but gives man the power to create and secure that which is wanted.

To master the organs of digestion would mean to keep those organs continually in such a perfect state of action that whatever the system needs could be digested perfectly, and without the slightest unpleasant sensation at any time or under any circumstance.

To master the heart does not mean that you can increase or decrease the heart-beats at will, but that you can keep the heart constantly in its true, normal action, no matter how much confusion or excitement there may be in your immediate environment.

The attainment of mastery, therefore, does not mean to interfere with natural action, but to promote natural action to the highest possible degree of perfection.

The idea of mastery is perfect action of all things at all times, regardless of circumstances or events. When you attain self-mastery, all things in your system will be doing their work perfectly, at all times, no matter what your work or your environment may be. And, in addition, this perfect action will constantly develop higher degrees of perfect action.

To master the elements and the forces of the system is not only to promote normal action in the chemical world, but to increase the quality and the power of that action by producing new and superior compounds.

Every mind forms different compounds, unconsciously, as the various grades of vibration are entered by the predominating mental states; but what is formed unconsciously is not always desirable, and when it is desirable it is always inferior to what might have been produced through a similar, intelligently directed conscious action.

Mental states of anger usually produce poisonous elements in the system, while states of fear and depression convert healthy tissues into useless, foreign matter. Such matter always clogs the system, thus interfering with natural functions, and producing, directly or indirectly, a number of ills.

Mental states that are lofty, true and constructive produce chemical compounds in the system that are nourishing and vitalizing, and that have a strong, refining tendency.

Through the power of self-mastery, undesirable compounds may be prevented entirely because the mind that masters self will not create other than wholesome mental states. Through the same power we may so direct and blend the elements of the system that the formation of the most beneficial and the most highly refined compounds may be constantly taking place.

The possibilities of this law are marvelous to say the least; it is through this law that false chemical conditions in the system may be transformed instantaneously into normal and wholesome actions, and it is through this law that all the elements of the physical body may be constantly refined, until absolute regeneration and spiritualization has taken place.

Through this law the physical body can be developed to the very highest degree of purity, wholeness, refinement and perfection, and made as beautiful as the Ideal Form itself. The application of this law, however, is possible only to those who have attained the mastery of self.

TO master the forces of the system, the principal object in view is to gain power to accumulate those forces in any part of mind or body where important work is to be done now; because, by giving all the power at hand now to the work we are doing now, that work will invariably result in a superior product.

To employ this method at all times would not only cause all things to be done well, but all things would constantly be done better, and failure would be a thing of the past.

If we would give the greater part of our active energy to the organs of digestion during meals, and for a short time after meals, we should never have anything but the most perfect digestion.

If we would give all the forces of intelligence and genius to the faculty that is in action now, that faculty would invariably do the work of genius, and would never fail to improve upon its own previous record.

The possibilities of self-mastery as applied to the forces of the system are therefore extraordinary; but we cannot master the forces of the system by trying to control those forces; to master any force, the will must act, not upon the force itself, but upon the interior cause of that force.

In the mastery of faculties, the purpose must be expansion and enlargement of conscious action; the average mind needs expansion of consciousness because most of its faculties are too small to give expression to all the energy of the system when concentration and accumulation take place. When this expansion has begun, however, quality, efficiency and volume may always be secured through the action of any faculty or talent.

Consequently, in the mental world one of the principal objects of self-mastery will be to lead consciousness into the realization of new and greater realms of perception and illumination, and to awaken a greater and greater measure of the great within.

The first real step in the mastery of self is to eliminate all desire to control what is exterior to yourself. Train your mind to desire only the mastery of your own being, and refuse absolutely to even think of controlling anything else. We cannot possibly master ourselves so long as there is the slightest desire to control others.

This may seem to be a contradiction of terms, because when one is master, he ought to be master of everything, whether it be in the without or in the within. But though mastery implies the mastery of everything, the fact must not be forgotten that the mastery of the without is simply an effect of the mastery of the within.

The mastery of environments, circumstances and external things, naturally follows when one has mastered himself; but so long as we try to control external things we cannot control ourselves, because we cannot produce causes while trying to interfere with effects.

The mastery of self can only be attained through the control of the inner side of mind, consciousness, thought and action; and to control the inner side constantly, the whole of attention must constantly be given to the inner side.

You control the exterior by causing the interior to become exactly what you wish the exterior to be.

The principle is, produce the cause you want and you will have the effect you want. The cause can be produced only by acting upon the subjective, because it is only the subjective side that has the power to originate cause; and to act upon the subjective, the forces of the mind must be trained to move towards the within.

However, whenever we try to control that which is exterior to ourselves, the forces of the mind will begin to move towards the without; and it is not possible for the forces of mind to go in while they are going out, neither can the tendency to act upon the within be established in mind so long as the outward movement of mind is permitted in the least.

The mind of the average person has already a strong tendency to move towards the surface, therefore to remove that tendency completely, the opposite tendency must be given the whole of attention; all the forces of mind must move towards the within at all times, and attention must be concentrated upon the subjective side absolutely without any cessation whatever.

It is not possible to form a tendency towards the inner life while the mind is acting more or less upon external things; a tendency is a continuous movement in a certain direction, therefore, while the mind is acting more or less upon the surface, the continuous movement towards the within will be interrupted and there will be no tendency towards the within.

We cannot train mental tendencies to move in opposite directions; no two forces, directly opposed to each other can exist in the mind at the same time.

If the entire mind is to be harmonious and constructive, all the forces of the mind must move towards the within; that is, they must move into the mind and not out of the mind. The person, however, who is trying to control external things while he is trying to develop the mastery of self, will cause his mind to be divided against itself. He will consequently control nothing.

When we realize the difference between the control of self and the control of others, and how they are direct opposites in purpose and action, we shall understand why the two cannot exist in the mind together. And since the methods employed in the control of persons and things are antagonistic to those employed in the control of self, it will not be possible to develop self-mastery so long as there is the least attempt to influence others.

It may seem impossible, however, to deal with other minds, especially with younger minds, without exercising some form of influence; but we must remember that there is a great difference between trying to control a mind and trying to instruct a mind.

To control a mind is to compel that mind to neglect its own power; to instruct a mind is to inspire in that mind the desire to use its own power.

To train another mind in the line of right thought and action, do not try to compel that mind to think right or act right; place before that mind ideas that will naturally produce right thought and right action.

And this can be done without having the slightest desire to influence or control.

It is upon this principle that the new education is based—the education that will not simply train small minds to remember what great minds have thought, but will train all small minds to become great minds.

GREAT is the mind that can leave everybody alone, that can be friendly to those who think what he cannot accept, and that can desire with his whole heart to have everybody be free to be themselves; but it is necessary to have such a mind if we would attain mastery of self.

If we are not to influence anyone it may be a problem to know how far we may go in persuading others to examine the desirability of the good things we have found in life. There is a natural tendency among us all to wish that everybody had all the good that we have, but we frequently go too far in trying to make people accept what they cannot appreciate. From this we observe that the human race is not depraved at all, but is somewhat lacking in judgment.

The best way and the simplest way to persuade others to take advantage of the good that you may have found, is to prove in your own life, that what you have found is better.

Never try to compel others to change; leave them free to change naturally and orderly because they want to; and they will want to change when they find that your change was worth while.

To inspire in others a desire to change for the better is truly noble; but this you can do only by leaving them alone, and becoming more noble yourself.

Make the most of yourself in your way, and leave everybody free to make the most of themselves in their way; they will when they find that it is better to enter the greater than to remain in the lesser; and that that is better you can prove by the way you live.

All minds want the best, and they will soon know the best when it is constantly before them as a living reality. People may not accept your theories, but if your life is better than theirs, they will soon do their utmost to live as you do.

After all, what would one have? Is it not life, the best life, the most beautiful life that we all seek?

To completely eliminate all desire to control persons and things, impress upon mind the great fact that it is not what others do but what you, yourself do, that determines whether good or ill shall come to you.

When this fact is realized, your one desire will be to perfect your own life, thought and action; you will find that the mastery of yourself will require all of your time and the whole of your attention, and you will interfere with others no more.

The true understanding of freedom will also help a great deal in removing the desire to interfere with others. When one finds that he cannot receive what he is not willing to give, and that so long as we deny freedom to others, others cannot give freedom to us, the relations between man and man become so clear that anyone can understand how to relate himself to the human race.

The best way, however, is to have so much faith in others that you know they will do the best they can without your telling them to do so. Such a faith may not always bring forth the best from everybody, but it will produce a strong tendency in that direction; and besides, it will make of you a superior being. You will advance constantly through such a faith, and thousands will follow your example.

To eliminate all desire to control others, however, is not the only essential; you must also eliminate all desire to control your own person. Nor is this a contradiction; to control the person you must act upon that inner power that can control the person; but it is not possible to act upon the power that is back of the person while attention is centered upon the person itself.

You cannot control the within while trying to control the without; the within is the world of cause, while the person is but the effect of what is being expressed from the inner cause.

As the subjective is, so is the objective;

the subjective is the inner life, and originates everything that appears in the objective or outer life.

We must not try to control the person, whether that person belongs to us or to some other soul.

True, we are to master the person, but we cannot master the person by concentrating attention upon the person; we master the person by expressing through the person those conditions and actions that we desire to see in the person, and those can be brought forth only from the within.

You can produce any change desired in the person by creating the cause of that change in the subconscious; and you can make the person express any desired action by creating the subconscious cause of that action. Nothing can be done, however, in the person, or through the person, unless the necessary cause is first produced in the subconscious, or what is frequently termed the subjective side of mind.

It is therefore evident that all effort to control the person or act upon the person, is wasted effort; results can be secured in the person only through that action that deals with the power back of the person, because what this power does, that the person will do also.

THE mastery of self implies the power to make the greatest and the best use of self, and to exercise this power is the real purpose of mastery; therefore, those mental states through which this power can act with the greatest efficiency must be cultivated.

The first essential mental state is harmony; complete and universal harmony, harmony with oneself, with everybody and with everything.

To be in harmony is to be properly related to that with which we may come in contact; and to be properly related to anything is to meet that something in its own world without disregarding the purpose of our world.

To be in harmony with everything is to adapt yourself to everything, and though this is an art requiring much thought and effort, it is absolutely necessary, because when one is not in harmony he is in discord, and discord misdirects energy.

To cultivate harmony, concentrate attention frequently upon the interior principle of harmony, the soul of harmony as it exists in the ideal within.

There is a state in the within that not

only is in harmony, but that is harmony; and to mentally grow in the consciousness of that state is to unfold the life of harmony throughout one's entire personality.

The second essential mental state is poise and its chief value in self mastery is the part it plays in holding together the energies of the system.

The mastery of self implies the possession of self, the conscious possession of one's entire self; that is, the holding together of the various activities, forces and elements in the system so that they may all work in unison in promoting the purpose the mind may now have in view. And this is poise.

Through the law of harmony you may change your mental attitudes at will, because when the consciousness of harmony is attained, you have not only the power to change your attitudes so as to harmonize yourself with everything, but you also discern instantaneously when to change, and in what way.

Through the law of poise, however, you gain the power to prevent mental change, which at times, and in a certain sense is absolutely necessary.

To be ever the same and yet never the same is to be on the perfect path to the greater life.

All the energies of the system must be held together in poise even when you are changing your mental attitudes to harmonize with something that is different.

Every change demands a law through which to produce its change; but this law does not change. The law is ever the same, and yet he who applies this law will be never the same.

The attitude of poise is the changeless attitude through which all energies must pass if constructive results and change for the better are to be secured. It is therefore indispensable to the attainment of self-mastery because to master the forces of the system is to have conscious possession of those forces, and that is poise.

To cultivate the attitude of poise, combine in consciousness the feeling of power and the feeling of peace. To feel immensely strong, and perfectly serene at the same time, is to be in poise.

The feeling of poise produces the feeling of self-possession, and to concentrate attention frequently upon our most perfect mental conception of the state of self-possession will develop the attitude of poise.

The third essential mental state is non-resistance; and the value of this state in the mastery of self is beyond measure.

To practice resistance is to direct attention upon the objective; it is trying to force things, and this causes the mind to act directly upon things; consciousness is brought to the surface, and the mental forces will begin to move towards the without instead of towards the within.

What we try to resist we try to control; and so long as we try to control anything we cannot attain the mastery of self.

The mental actions of resistance employ the external will altogether, something that must be eliminated completely before mastery can take place.

The external will, that is, ordinary will-power, is one of the principal obstacles to the attainment of self-mastery, and so long as we practice resistance this will-power will live and grow.

The stronger the power of the ordinary will, the larger will be the time required to attain the mastery of self, unless that form of will-power is eliminated completely at the beginning.

Resistance, however, is the chief pro-moter of this form of will-power; therefore, non-resistance must be made the one great rule in everything, whether in life, thought or action.

To practice resistance is to try to overcome by going against; to practice non-resistance is to overcome by going above. Resistance wastes its energy by fighting what it does not want; non-resistance leaves behind what it does not want and proceeds serenely to employ its energy in creating what it does want.

It is therefore evident that resistance never can succeed, while non-resistance always does succeed.

To enter the attitude of non-resistance is not to bring your life to a standstill, nor to fold your arms, permitting persons, circumstances and things to do to you what they like. Non-resistance is a forward movement, while resistance is never anything but retrogression.

The non-resisting mind does not antagonize the wrongs that are behind, and all wrongs are behind, but proceeds in peace to realize the greater good that is before.

The attitude of non-resistance makes man a stronger individuality, and he who becomes stronger will not remain in the hands of the weaker.

To resist what is against us is to continue to be small, and he who is small cannot overcome those obstacles that may seem to be great.

Resistance scatters and wastes energy; non-resistance accumulates and constructively employs energy. Therefore to practice the former is to remain weak, while to practice the latter is to develop strength and power in greater and greater measure.

To use your power in resisting wrongs is

to continue in bondage to those wrongs, because we give our power to that which we resist. To use your power for self-development and self-mastery is to rise superior to every circumstance and condition, which means inevitable victory and complete emancipation.

THE fourth essential mental state is receptivity, or the attitude of responsiveness—that attitude that places the mind in perfect touch with everything that it may desire to receive.

The objective or personal life is controlled by causing the objective to respond to the subjective, and there is positively no other law through which the person may be controlled.

It is not necessary to act upon the person to control the person, nor would such action produce any results whatever; the person will respond only to that which is taking place in the within, therefore, to create the desired subjective action, and train the person to respond to that action, is to secure the desired objective action.

The mastery of the personal self depends entirely upon the degree of responsiveness that exists in the person; but how can responsiveness be cultivated in the person if we are not to act upon the person? And if this quality is developed from within, how can the person, in the beginning, respond even to responsiveness?

The fact is that receptivity has its existence primarily in consciousness, and as con-

.

sciousness fills the personal self, everything that is developed in consciousness will be active in the person.

When you become conscious of the state of receptivity, the person will respond to everything with which you may come in contact, whether the contact be with the without or with the within.

The receptive mind is easily influenced and affected by everything, both good and otherwise; for this reason, no mind should place itself in sympathetic contact with environments that are contrary to its own ideals.

What enters mind from adverse environments or inferior associations will manifest in the person according to the degree of receptivity that may be present at the time; but since it is possible to control the attitude of receptivity so that we come in mental contact only with that which is desirable, every person may determine what he is to receive, and what he is not to receive, from the physical or mental worlds in which he may be living now.

The power that environment may exercise in the life of any person depends entirely upon himself, how receptive he may happen to be; but since anyone can train himself to respond only to those things that are superior to himself, he may eliminate completely every form of influence that may come from those circumstances, persons or things that are inferior.

It is absolutely necessary that the person should respond to the mind if it is to be mastered by the mind, but since the person, when highly receptive, will respond to everything that enters the mind, nothing that is inferior or undesirable must be permitted to enter the mind.

To prevent this, however, another, and a corresponding state of mind, viz., positiveness, must be cultivated.

The person that is not receptive is barely alive, and can accomplish nothing of real value; receptivity is, therefore, indispensable, and the fact that the receptive person responds to that which is not good, as well as to that which is good, should not cause any hesitancy in the cultivation of receptivity.

The person does not respond directly to anything that exists in the without, but only to that which has first entered the mind, and the mind has the power to select from every source what it wants to accept, and reject what it does not wish to use.

To cultivate the state of receptivity, encourage the actions of the finer forces and the finer vibrations in the system. Whenever these forces are felt, the mind should become quiet and should enter more deeply into the feeling of those forces.

It is the finer forces to which the person responds, therefore, to promote the development of receptivity the action of these forces should be increased perpetually through the entire personality.

Another essential to the cultivation of receptivity is to enter into the closest possible mental touch with the finer elements that permeate all things; mentally live with the soul of things; and this is the true receptivity.

When we realize the great value of receptivity, and find that the person can respond to the low as well as to the high, it becomes necessary to find a method through which this delicate faculty may be so guarded and directed that it will respond only to the superior.

In other words how shall the mind protect itself from being impressed with the many inferior things with which we come in daily contact?

What we see, hear or feel, or meet in any way, produces some impression upon the mind; in fact, everything that enters through the senses will impress the mind, and every impression, if sufficiently strong, will affect the mind, and then the person.

We cannot close our eyes to what we see; we must, therefore, find a method through which we may prevent what we do see from impressing the mind when we so elect.

We want all our senses to be thoroughly

alive, and we want consciousness to be wide-awake to everything that is taking place in our present state of existence, but we also want the power to close the mental door to every impression from without that is not worthy of being entertained.

This power is found in the state of positiveness, the fifth essential mental state.

So long as the mind is in a positive state, nothing can impress the mind unless that impression is deeply desired, and the reason why is simple.

It is the creative energies of mind that produce the mental impressions, but these energies will do only what they are directed to do by the vibrations that enter the mind. These vibrations may come from without, through the senses, or they may come from within, through the mind's own thinking, and the creative energies will obey those vibrations that have the greatest power.

When the vibrations from without are the strongest, as is the case in the average mind, the creative energies will proceed to form impressions, states, conditions and thoughts that are exactly similar to the ideas that are being conveyed by the vibrations from without; and the mental world will be created in the likeness of the exterior environment.

However, when the mind is in a positive state, the vibrations from within are the strongest, and no vibration from without can produce an impression upon the mind unless the mental door is consciously opened to that particular idea.

When you are in a positive state, nothing that you may see, hear or feel will impress your mind unless you so desire. It is therefore evident that so long as you remain in a positive state, you will never be controlled by environments, circumstances, persons or things.

Positiveness is that state wherein the mind generates its own vibrations and its own mental life; forms its own mental attitudes, thinks consciously its own thoughts, and is so strong in its own individualized being that no power can act in the mental domain unless it is wanted.

To be positive, however, does not mean to domineer over anything, but to feel the fullness of invincible life and power, and to fill the mind with the fullness of that life and power.

You do not have to exercise control over the forces of the mind; you do not have to compel the creative energies to ignore the vibrations, the influences and the ideas that come from without; it is simply necessary to fill your own mind with your own mental vibrations, and to make those vibrations stronger than those that may try to enter from without.

So long as you fill yor r mind with your

own mental vibrations, and you always do when in a positive state, the creative energies will produce only those thoughts and impressions that you desire to have produced; the desires of your own true self will be obeyed by the powers within you, and those desires alone.

The value of positiveness lies, first, in its power to protect the mind from being impressed by inferior, external conditions; and secondly, in its power to keep the creative energies under the complete control of the mind.

The positive mind has the power to think whatever it may want to think, and this is the real secret of the mastery of self.

He alone can master himself who can master his mind; and he alone can master his mind who can think what he wants to think, at any time and under any circumstance.

To develop positiveness, simply be positive at all times; that is the whole secret, and it is something that any one can do with perfect ease.

Feel the fullness of invincible life and power, and fill your mind with this life and power. Resist nothing, domineer over nothing, and try to control nothing. Feel positively that you are a master, because that is what you are.

The sixth essential mental state to the

Sorry:
The defect on the previous page was that way in the original book we reproduced.

attainment of the mastery of self, is the consciousness of superiority.

It is not possible to attain self-mastery so long as one thinks that he is an inferior creature, because through that thought mind goes down and functions below its true level.

We can control only that which we have risen above, therefore, no mastery is possible until we live in the mental world of superiority.

The idea, however, is not that we are to think of ourselves as being superior to others, we know that the same superiority that exists in us exists in every person, and it is this superiority into which we desire to enter.

The idea is to dwell constantly upon the mountain top of your being; to live consciously and perpetually at the very apex of all your aspirations, and to constantly function in the most perfect spheres of those present possibilities that you can now realize.

The purpose of self-mastery is to make all of life just as high as our highest vision of the ideal; and we have attained mastery when we can make everything in life become exactly what we wish it to be.

The act of mastering oneself implies the power to bring oneself up to the state of superiority; to make everything superior to what it was, and then press on to still greater heights.

The purpose of mastery is not to control

faculties, talents, forces or elements, but to direct them all towards greater attainments and greater achievements—towards superiority.

It is not possible, however, to cause everything in one's being to move towards superiority unless the mind is established in the consciousness of superiority; to produce mental tendencies towards the superior, consciousness must feel the life, the spirit and the soul of the superior, and this feeling may be cultivated by frequently concentrating attention upon the most perfect conception of superiority that the mind can possibly form.

Whatever we frequently think of, with depth and feeling, that we shall gain the consciousness of; this is a law through which any hidden secret may be brought into the light of a clear, positive understanding.

The seventh essential mental state is the realization of supremacy; the knowing of the truth that you, yourself, are the supreme ruler over everything in your being and in your world.

We must remove the idea of exercising control over the person through the use of objective will-power, and in the place of that idea establish the realization of supremacy.

When one knows that he is the supreme master of his being, he rules supremely without trying to do so; and herein we learn why he who has attained the mastery of self never tries to master or control anything, not even himself.

It is not necessary to try to be that which you are; and as you are created with the power to master yourself, you do not have to try, at any time, to master yourself. You are the supreme master of your being, and to think the truth, you must think of yourself as such.

He *is* what he is who knows that he *is;* and he who knows *what* he is, does what he *can* do by the virtue of being what he *is.*

He who knows that he is supreme in his own being exercises supremacy by the virtue of being supreme.

He who is supreme cannot do otherwise but exercise supremacy; and since man is supreme in his own being he must necessarily exercise supremacy in his own being; that is, when he knows that he is what he *is.*

Man in the real is a master; therefore, when in the consciousness of the real, he does master; and does not have to try. He who tries to be a master does not know that he really is a master; when he knows that he is, he will do that which he has the power to do, not by trying, but by doing what he is in being.

The sun does not try to shine; it is light;

therefore, it does shine. The sun does not have to control the sunbeams; the sun creates the sunbeams by being the cause of sunbeams; the sunbeams are created to give light because they proceed from that which is light; and that which is created to give light will give light because it is light; it will not have to be controlled to do so.

A piece of ice *is* cold, therefore, it makes everything cold with which it comes in contact; it does not have to try to produce cold. It is not necessary for any force or element in nature to try to produce in itself that which already exists in itself; neither is it necessary for man to try to do this.

So long as we try to master ourselves we shall not succeed in mastering anything; but when we discover that we in truth *are* masters, we shall succeed in mastering everything without trying in the least to do so.

The realization of supremacy is therefore of the highest value, because this realization will reveal man to himself. He will *know* that he is supreme in his own being; he will know that he is created with that power, and when man knows what he is he will act accordingly.

To cultivate the mental state of supremacy, impress the mind as frequently as possible with the truth that you are supreme in your own being. If you were not, you could not exist; your being would be chaos; the fact that you exist as an individualized entity proves that you are supreme in the being of that entity, and to be just to yourself you must exercise the whole of that power.

Therefore, to impress the mind with the idea that you are supreme in your being, is simply to train your mind to understand a great truth; and when that truth is realized, the realization of supremacy will have been attained; you will know what you are and you will act with supremacy in everything that is done within yourself.

When the mind acts with supremacy in the within, all the creations of mind will be patterned after the highest ideals that may now exist in consciousness; and the progress of the individual will be remarkable.

The reason why so many fail to reach their ideals is because they do not act with supremacy in the inner world of creation; they, therefore, do not recreate themselves in the likeness of their ideals, and no person can realize his ideals until he grows into the exact likeness of those ideals.

When the mind has not attained the consciousness of supremacy it cannot act with supremacy; the creative energies will, consequently, follow lower ideals, and will not do what is wanted done.

To enter fully into the consciousness of

supremacy, all knowledge that reveals the
unlimited possibilities of man will prove of
great value, because the more deeply we can
penetrate the greatness already existing
within us, the more firmly we can establish
the consciousness of supremacy.

To constantly feel that one is supreme in
his own domain is absolutely necessary, and
as this feeling would simply be the conscious
expression of what is the truth, no one
should hesitate for a moment to enter that
attitude, and to dwell therein forever.

The person may feel weak, but that does
not prove that you are weak; the weakness
of the person is felt because you have failed
to bring forth your own real strength.

Know that you are strong, and all weakness will disappear; know that you are
supreme in your own domain, and you will
rule supremely in your own domain. You
will rule with supreme power because you
are the individualization of supreme power.

AVING established the mind in the seven states that are necessary to the attainment of self-mastery, the next essential is to train the will to perform its true function.

To begin, we must discard the current belief that the will was made to rule; the very opposite is its function; the true will never attempts to rule anything, but holds itself constantly in that attitude through which it can be ruled by the mind's highest conception of law, principle and truth.

Man attains self-mastery not by trying to rule, but by permitting himself to be ruled by that which is greater than his present conception of himself.

That personality is always the most powerful that lets go of its own personal power and gives itself up completely to superior power.

He who is willing to lose the smaller life for the sake of the larger, will gain the larger; and he who is willing to lose his limited personal power for the sake of unlimited impersonal power, will gain the unlimited.

In like manner, he who disposes of the will that tries to rule, for the sake of the will that is *the* ruler, will receive the latter, which is the real will. And this is necessary, because the mastery of self cannot be attained so long as will-power is exercised in the usual way.

The true will never tries to rule, it already is the ruling power; and it never tries to gain supremacy; it already is supreme.

Since the true will already is supreme, it would be a misuse of will to try to become supreme. Through such actions an inferior imitation of the real will would be employed, and that imitation would not contain any will-power whatever, but would simply be some aimless use of superficial mental force.

What is usually termed the personal will, that is, that something that we employ when we try to rule or domineer, is not will-power in any form; the personal will is nothing but the misuse of mental forces.

In the average person the real will is never employed; what passes for will in those minds is a more or less uncertain expression of those states of consciousness that have gained some imperfect conception of the real will.

Through every mental conception of the will a temporary state of consciousness is established having a tendency to direct, and to take initial steps. This is natural, because since the will itself is the ruling power every mental conception of the will would have a tendency to rule.

Each mental conception of the will bears a slight resemblance to the will, and receives a tendency to act accordingly. Consequently, a mental conception of the will, by virtue of this slight resemblance, imitates the will with imperfect attempts to rule.

When we take initial steps, we are said to use the will, but we do not; we simply express our latest mental conception of the will; and since all such conceptions have tendencies to rule, direct, or take initial steps, initial steps, however imperfect, will accordingly be taken.

It is the truth, well known to everybody, that the average initial step is a mistake; and it could not very well be otherwise, because it is not taken by the real will, but by an inferior imitation. It is also well known that most of our attempts at exercising the power to rule are complete failures and lead both object and subject into confusion.

It is also the truth, easily demonstrated, that practically all the mistakes of the world come originally from the tendency of the mind to follow imitations of the will instead of the real will itself.

The ills of life are wholly due to the mistakes we make when trying to control and direct our actions by the personal will; while the great and the good things that are done are done only when the mind gives way to a superior power, and acts under the direction and inspiration of the supreme will.

The pronounced individualist may object to the idea that we are to give up to a superior power, but such objections will disappear when we realize that this superior power is our own power, and that we are simply discarding the false and the limited in order that we may take possession of the limitless and the true.

In like manner, all objections to the idea that the will must place itself in that attitude where it can be ruled by the superior, will disappear when we realize that through that attitude of the will, the will is permitted to be itself.

In order that the will may be itself, it should make no effort to rule, but should remain what it is—*the power that does rule.*

The will is properly performing its true function when it is eternally giving away to the superior; that is, the superior that is in itself, that is in man, and that is in the expression of the infinite in man.

The true function of the will is to hold the mind in such a state that the higher may find a full and free expression at all times. In other words, to keep the mind open to the perpetual influx of life and power from on high—that is what the true will is created to do; and that is sufficient; the mind that is constantly being filled with the superior, will receive everything that it may desire to receive because the superior contains everything.

Such a mind will also become what it may wish to become, because to be filled with the superior is to become superior. It will also achieve anything that may be undertaken, because there is no limit to the power from which the superior eternally proceeds.

The difference, therefore, between the real will and its man-made imitations is immense, and any one can understand that man has nothing to lose and everything to gain by eliminating the latter and giving up completely to the power of the former.

THE purpose of the personal will is to try to compel things to do thus or so; but this is not necessary, neither can anything but undesirable results proceed from such efforts.

Things will do that which they are created to do when left to themselves; and since everything has the inherent right to be itself and itself only, we can not try to make them do or be different without violating the law of freedom.

When we desire different things we should cause different things to be created, and not try to make things already created different from what they are. This, however, is constantly being done; the result is, we not only misplace things, but we interfere, more or less, with the natural inclinations and best motives of nearly every person with whom we came in contact.

This practice leads to the violation of the law of freedom on every hand, and since we can not expect to receive from others what we do not wish to give to others, there can be no freedom for ourselves until we interfere with persons and things no more.

The leading purpose of the personal will

is to change things in the without; to try to make over what has already been created. In brief, the ordinary will-power is simply a meddler, and is engaged principally in the work of interference, trying to prevent persons and things from being themselves.

This purpose, however, is contrary to all the laws of life, because the very first principle in life is to give everything the freedom to be what it is.

When we wish to change things we must not misplace them, but proceed to transmute them; and transmutation is brought about, not by interfering with the present external condition of things, but through the expression of superior power into the interior life of things.

When things are not as they should be, we can change them, not by trying to remake the present external condition of things, but by creating a new internal condition for things.

We remove evil, not by resistance nor by interference, but by permitting evil to be itself, which is nothing. Evil, being mere nothingness or emptiness, would never disturb us if we did not make "something" out of it.

The more we interfere with evil the more we make of evil and the more we disturb the development of the good, thus retarding the growth of the very thing that *can* remove evil.

We can not remove evil; this the good alone can do; but we can create the good in sufficient abundance to cause all evil to disappear.

We have no time to create the good while constantly interfering with evil; and since it is the creation of the good and the good alone that can remove evil, we understand perfectly why we should not disturb the tares.

We have given ages of time to the pulling up of tares, but there are just as many tares in the world now as there ever were. Nothing has been gained; we have not removed the ills of life by constantly interfering with those ills; the method is a complete failure, and should be abandoned absolutely.

It can be demonstrated conclusively that evil invariably disappears when left to itself, to be itself, which is nothing; but to leave evil alone, the mind must give the whole of its attention to the creation of the good.

The personal will, however, can not leave evil alone; its nature is to interfere; therefore, it must be eliminated, and the entire mind placed absolutely in the hands of Supreme Will.

When we compare, briefly, the two methods for dealing with adverse conditions, we find that the old method, the method of the personal will, through a constant interference with evil, never succeeds in eliminating evil, while the new method, through a constant creation of the good, soon eliminates all the evil there is.

Employ the new method, and evil will continue but a short time, and it is no more; but so long as the old method is employed, evil will live and grow, with no promise of cessation whatever.

When we examine evil we find that it is a condition of emptiness or incompleteness, and can live only until the fullness and the completeness of the opposite good appears.

The harvest of tares, which we have been told not to prevent, is therefore not some future fixed time, but any time when the true life-forces of growth are made sufficiently strong to bring evil conditions to an end.

This end can be brought about by any person, in his own life, at any time, by the giving of all his power and the whole of his attention to the creation of those good things that are necessary to fill the conditions of nothingness that may exist in the world.

The harvest of tares, that is, the end of evil conditions in any personal life, can be produced at once, and complete emancipation secured now; but the personal will must first give way to the ruling power of the real will.

To use the will for the purpose of interfer-

ing with things, as they are, not only per-
petuates evil, but also prevents everything
in life from being its best.

Nothing can be its best unless it is given
freedom to be itself, its true and complete
self; and in order that we may enter that
attitude wherein we naturally give all things
the freedom to be themselves, we must
permit both the perfect and the imperfect to
be what they are.

Our tendency to interfere with the imperfect will disappear of itself when we realize
that the imperfect will not pass away until
we create something better to take its place.

However, to create that something better
it is necessary to attain a higher understanding of the superior, and also to bring into
action the finer creative forces. The present
states of mind must give place to states that
have all the essentials required for the creation of the better; but this becomes possible
only when the will is employed in its true
function.

**T**HE purpose of self-mastery is the attainment of superiority; to employ all the elements of being in such a way that perpetual growth becomes the principal factor in existence.

You have attained mastery of all the forces and elements of your being when you have caused all of these to work together constantly for the higher development of your entire self.

To simply make certain forces in your system obey your desires does not indicate any degree of self-mastery; in fact, every attempt to control your forces according to personal desires will pervert the will, and thus prevent the attainment of mastery. But when any force has been made constructive and constructive only, then you are the master of that force.

It is the true purpose of all forces to be constructive; they are, therefore, not in their true sphere of action until they have become permanently constructive; and he who has accomplished this has mastered the powers of his being.

To master yourself is to cause all things in yourself to enter their true sphere of action, and the very moment that the will proceeds to direct all things in being into their true spheres of action, the first step in mastership has been attained.

The will cannot direct things, however, until it has given up completely to that superior power that is the ruling power; and its direction of things into their true spheres of action consists in the placing of things in the hands of this same power.

When analyzing the true will and its true function, we find that its one and only purpose is to act upon consciousness; not to control consciousness, but to act upon consciousness.

The will was not made to act upon the body, nor upon any of the forces and elements in the body; neither was it made to act upon the mind, nor upon any of the states, the tendencies or the desires of the mind.

The will should act upon consciousness only, and the reason why is found in the fact that everything that appears in body or mind is but the effect of conscious states.

Whatever you become conscious of, that you will express in the personality, and mind and body will become what those expressions are. The conditions of those expressions will be externalized in the personality, and the person will feel, act and behave exactly as those expressions feel, act and behave.

Every change that actually takes place in

consciousness will produce a corresponding change in the personality, and every step in advance that is realized in consciousness will cause the personality to advance and develop in a similar manner.

Every cause that is formed in consciousness will produce its own effect in the personality, and as any cause desired may be produced in consciousness, any effect desired may be secured in mind or body.

There is nothing, however, except the true will that can produce causes in consciousness, therefore the will must be trained for this work.

In training the will for practical purposes, the mind should be centered as much as possible upon the true function of the will; the personal will should be ignored completely, and no thought whatever should be given to the exercise of control over anything, nor should the slightest desire to rule be permitted.

To feel a desire to rule, control, antagonize or resist, means that the true will is not recognized, and that the mind is permitting itself to be misled by inferior imitations.

The true will always moves towards the superior; it acts upon consciousness for the purpose of causing consciousness to gain a higher and a larger conception of the superior, and as these superior conceptions are realized in mind, they become patterns for the creative energies. Superior thoughts, desires, tendencies, actions and conditions will thereby be created throughout the entire system.

The will is created to take the initial step in everything that transpires in human existence; and since all the elements of life follow the will, it is of the highest importance that every step be a step in advance, because if it is not, the elements of life will produce the inferior; retrogression will then take place and the very things that are not wanted will appear in life.

However, when the will is true every step that is taken will be a step in advance, a step towards the consciousness of greater superiority; the true will is superior, therefore can will to act only in the life of superiority.

The will is superior now; it is above all other functions and attributes; nothing takes place until the will acts; it is the master over all, and therefore occupies the highest place in mind. Consequently, when we recognize the will in its true state, we recognize something that is superior, and all our thoughts will ascend towards the superior.

When all the actions of mind are moving towards the superior, greatness is being developed and the purpose of mastery is being fulfilled.

We master any particular part of the

system when that part is made to perform its true function under all sorts of conditions; and we further master the same part when we have trained it to perform its function much better than it ever did before.

To cause this perfect action, and the more perfect action, to take place in any particular part of the system, this action must first be caused in consciousness, because each part of the system simply carries out what consciousness holds for it to do. The various forces, elements, organs and states are mere channels of expression for conscious action.

Change a certain phase of consciousness, and the corresponding mental or physical expression changes likewise; but no change can possibly take place in any part of the personality until the necessary change is produced in consciousness; and nothing can produce this change in consciousness but the true action of the true will.

The prevailing state of consciousness is the only one cause in the personal being of man; all other things are effects of this one cause; it is therefore useless for the will to act upon anything else but consciousness because it is only through consciousness that the purpose of the will can be promoted.

To train the will to will in harmony with the real will, form in mind a clear conception of the real will; then will only the larger, the higher and the better.

As the consciousness of the real will is developed, the will-power becomes immensely strong; and there are two reasons why; first, because the true will does not destroy its strength through the desire to rule; and second, because it gives itself up to the influx of real power—the power that proceeds from the source of limitless power.

As this power fills the system more and more, a deep stillness is gained, a state of being that is not only perfectly serene, but immensely strong; peace and power united; and when this state of being is felt, one may know that the path to self-mastery has been found.

To enter this state is to begin the mastery of self, and to continue in this state is to continue to develop the mastery of self to the very highest possible degree.

To step outside of this state is to cease, for the time being, to master oneself, and herein one may know whether he is on the path to mastery or not.

To hold the mind and every part of the mind in this serene, strong state, and to hold it there at all times, is a very high art, and is made possible only through the training of the will to act upon the principle of the real will.

When the will wills to be what it *is*—the ruling power, and wills to feel the action of this power, the mind will enter the strong, serene state, because the action of the real will is perfectly serene, and its power is immensely strong.

TO MASTER oneself is to cause oneself to be what one wishes to be. To eternally become what one desires to become means a perpetual transformation of self because all becoming is change —eternal change for the better; and to perpetually transform the self, a higher order of life and thought must be constantly expressed in the self.

This, however, is made possible only through the awakening of higher and larger states of consciousness, and as consciousness responds only to the actions of the will, the true use of the will becomes indispensable in the attainment of the mastery of self.

To train the will to act upon consciousness, will-power should be concentrated upon every individualization of consciousness in the personality as well as upon consciousness in general.

If we wish to produce a certain effect in any part of the personality, the will should act upon the consciousness that permeates that part, and the cause that can produce the desired effect should be impressed upon that state of consciousness.

Consciousness permeates every atom in your entire being, and every atom responds to the action of that part of consciousness that is centered within the atom; it is therefore possible to produce any desired physical or chemical effect in any part of the personality by producing in the consciousness within that part the desired cause.

There is a special center of consciousness in every organ of the body, and in every faculty of the mind; therefore, to produce any desired effect upon any special organ or faculty, the will must act, not upon the organ or faculty itself, but upon the center of consciousness that is within that organ or faculty.

The reason why the average person fails to control his body or mind is because he uses will-power upon the body and the mind instead of upon the consciousness that permeates both.

Control the consciousness that permeates the body and you control the body as well; and consciousness is readily controlled when the will acts directly upon consciousness while strongly desiring to secure certain results.

To cause the will to act directly upon consciousness, concentrate attention upon the finest substance or life that you can picture as permeating that part of mind or body where you desire the effect to be produced.

To illustrate, when concentrating upon the

73

brain do not think of the brain itself, nor use will-power upon the brain, but turn will and attention upon the finer life-forces that permeate the brain. Likewise when concentrating upon any organ in the body, do not direct the will upon the physical organ, but upon the finer forces that permeate that organ. In this way you will act directly upon the center of consciousness within that organ, and whatever you impress that center of consciousness to do, the organ itself will do.

Through the same process the center of consciousness in any organ or faculty may be so strongly individualized that it will respond instantaneously to any action that may be made by the will. The stronger the center of consciousness in any part of the personality the stronger the subconscious action of the will in that center; and as it is the subconscious action of the will that controls, the value of developing strong centers of consciousness in every part of the personality becomes evident.

When attention is being concentrated upon the various centers of consciousness, the will must never try to control those centers, or domineer, in any way, over consciousness itself. The object of the will is to impress upon consciousness those actions or qualities that are desired in personal expression.

To promote this object, the force of will and the force of desire should be combined into one action, and this action should be directed where results are to be secured.

The true will and the true desire are the two halves of the same whole; they are therefore indispensable to each other, and the more thoroughly they are trained to work as one, the sooner will the mastery of self be attained.

Desire receives, and the will directs action upon the object that the mind wishes to receive. Before the mind can receive, consciousness must come in contact with the object desired, and to direct consciousness into that contact, the will is required, because the will is the only power that can direct.

When desire acts without the will, it fails to bring consciousness into contact with the object desired; nothing is therefore received; and this explains why most desires are never fulfilled.

When the will acts without desire, the mental attitude that receives and appropriates is absent; there is no receptivity, therefore, nothing is received; and this explains why mere will-power is powerless to gain the object in view.

When the will acts upon a certain state of consciousness, there should be a very strong desire to awaken into positive action

75

what may be latent in that state; and, conversely, whenever the mind feels a strong desire for something, the will should act directly upon the inner or subjective state of that center of consciousness that contains that something.

Through these methods, what we desire to receive will be received, and what we will to accomplish will be accomplished.

The desire that is aimless, and the will that domineers but never directs—these two actions in mind are responsible for nearly all the failures in life; it is therefore evident that failure could be reduced to a minimum in every sphere of life when the force of desire and the force of will were combined into one perfect action.

Such an action would be irresistible, and would invariably gain what it willed and desired to gain. It would be the action of complete mastery wherever it willed and desired to act.

We may desire power for ages, but so long as consciousness is not placed in touch with the inner source of power, we shall desire in vain. We can receive nothing from any source, until we place mind in contact with that source, and to produce that contact, the will must direct consciousness to become conscious of that source.

It is the truth that we may gain possession of anything in the external world that we may require, if we unfold the necessary capacity and ability from the internal world; but again, it is only the true use of the will, combined with a strong desire, that can place mind in touch with the limitless power of this internal ability.

To use will-power without desire is to stupify the mind; and here we have one reason why so many minds lack brilliancy.

To use desire without will is to place the mind in a negative state, where it may be controlled by anything that may appear in its environment.

To combine the force of will and the force of desire into one action, no particular method is required, except to will to desire whatever you desire to desire, and to desire to accomplish whatever you will to accomplish.

Whenever you desire to unfold and express a certain condition, state or quality in your being, cause the will to act upon the inner consciousness of that condition, state or quality; and when you employ the will in any way whatever, desire something definite at the time, with the very strongest desire that you can possibly arouse.

When causing the will to act upon consciousness, think of the soul of things; consciousness is always reached when attention is concentrated upon the *soul* of things, because consciousness is that finer something that permeates the soul of things. It has neither shape nor form, yet it is *in* all shapes and forms.

WHAT is termed the soul of things is the inner world of limitless possibility; therefore, by causing will and desire to act upon the inner world of consciousness, the greater things that are latent within are unfolded, developed and expressed.

We thereby train ourselves to promote the purpose of self-mastery to a greater and a greater degree, because we attain the mastery of self only by eternally bringing forth a superior self.

It is therefore evident that every attempt towards self-mastery must have the superior self always in view; and this is accomplished perfectly when the forces of will and desire act invariably upon the inner consciousness of everything in the human system.

When the self is perfect, as far as its present requirements are concerned, it needs no control; it will be right and do right because it is right. When a certain organ in the body performs its function perfectly, it needs no attention; it needs no control in order that it may do its work; it is already subconsciously controlled by its own state of harmony with the real will.

It is the same with everything in the system; no mastery is needed over anything while it is doing its work perfectly, because it is already in the hands of mastery; but if it is not doing its work perfectly, it needs transformation, not control.

You cannot control the wrong to be right; but you can transmute and transform the wrong into the right; you can gradually transform the inferior into the superior, and it has been demonstrated that when the entire system is being steadily transformed, every part of the system will not only perform its function properly, but will perpetually improve the work of that function.

The best way to keep the entire system in order, is to constantly improve the entire system; and this is the purpose of self-mastery.

To master self is not to try to control self, but to perpetually transform self; it means continuous advancement for every part of the being of man; it is the elimination of evil through a constant growth in the realization of the good; it is overcoming the imperfect by creating the perfect; it is the passing out of the lesser through the passing into the greater; it is the prevention of retrogression through the perpetual promotion of progression.

The law of continuous advancement, however, is based upon the principle that every change or improvement that is to be produced in life must come from the unfoldment of the greater possibilities that are latent in life. We advance in the without by unfolding and expressing the greater from the within; and we master the self by causing the self to eternally become what is latent in the superior life within the self.

The mastery of self may therefore be promoted only through the practical application of this principle; that is, every action of mind, desire or will must act upon the greater within. Before a desired effect can be secured in the without, the corresponding cause must be created in the within; and to create this cause, action must be concentrated upon the consciousness of the within.

To control the forces of the system, the mind, through the united action of will and desire, must act upon the finer forces that permeate the finer elements throughout the system. Produce any desired impression upon the finer forces while mentally entering into the inner world of the finer forces, and the outer forces of the personality will act exactly as the impression desired.

Discord, confusion, irritability, restlessness or pain among the forces of the system can be removed instantaneously by impressing upon the finer forces the desire for peace, serenity, harmony and poise.

When the mind enters the finer forces while in the attitude of harmony, perfect harmony will immediately be established throughout the personality.

This is how adverse conditions in the system may be mastered; not by trying to control those conditions, but by entering into the finer consciousness and creating there more perfect conditions.

Whenever you wish to change physical action, direct attention upon the subjective side, that is, the finer consciousness that permeates that part of the physical form through which the new action is to appear, and desire that subjective side to act the way you wish the physical part to act; and as soon as the desired subjective action is produced the corresponding physical action will immediately follow.

In this way, the body can be controlled completely, and caused to act in any way that we may desire.

To remove physical pain or disease, concentrate attention upon the finer consciousness of that part of the body where the pain is felt. Do not think of the body itself, nor the ailment, but cause the mind to enter into the finer elements and the finer forces that permeate that part of the body where the adverse condition appears.

While in the attitude of concentration, use the will in drawing all the forces of that part of the body into the finer vibrations, and desire, with deep feeling, to realize the health and the wholeness of this finer life into which the mind has entered.

The reaction will soon follow, and the adverse condition will be caused to disappear by the coming forth of a strong, wholesome life from within.

Every unpleasant sensation in the physical system can be removed by refining the vibrations in those parts where the sensations are felt; and the vibrations of any part of the system will be refined when attention is concentrated upon the finer forces that permeate those parts.

To master your mental attitudes, turn attention upon the silent within. There is a state in the inner field of consciousness where absolute peace prevails at all times; to become conscious of this state is to become calm and serene, and by directing attention upon this state the realization of peace will immediately follow.

When in the midst of confusion, do not permit your mental forces to run towards the surface; to do this is to become confused, and thus be controlled by the confusion that exists about you.

Draw all your mental forces towards the within, while in such surroundings, and think towards the peaceful within; you will thereby realize peace, and be in peace. You will master yourself in the midst of the storm; you will remain untouched, unmoved and undisturbed.

To control your thoughts, do not try to control those thoughts that you are thinking now, but use the will in producing a new line of thinking. If the will is well trained this can be done at once, and as the mind becomes active in new fields of consciousness, those thoughts that we did not wish to entertain will disappear of themselves.

To think of something different becomes simplicity itself when the mind enters into the finer consciousness of new thought. It is only when the mind continues to act upon the surface that it is difficult to change the mind.

To control your feelings, enter into the finer feeling of the opposite states of feeling. Having decided upon the way you want to feel, turn attention upon the finer consciousness of the state of feeling desired. The desired state will soon be felt in every part of the system.

To control desires, transmute the forces that are trying to express themselves through those desires; then turn the transmuted energy into those parts of mind or body where expression may legitimately take place now.

To transmute the energies that are alive in any desire, concentrate attention upon that part of mind or body where the desire is centralized, and with the action of desire and will draw all the finer forces of that part towards the subjective side.

When the finer forces are felt, attention may be turned upon any part of the body or into any faculty where added power can be used with profit. Wherever attention is directed, there the finer forces will accumulate, that is, when the consciousness of those forces has been attained.

Through this same process all the finer elements and forces in the personality or the mentality may be called into action, and superior results secured in everything one may undertake to do.

All the forces of the system are creative, and the creative process may be promoted anywhere in the system by any of the forces of the system; therefore, if the creative function cannot now take place in the personality, the same force may be employed now in any part of the mentality. This being true, it is wasted effort to try to subdue one's physical passions; when physical desires are felt, and it is not possible to express them physically at the time, the force of those desires should be transmuted, and concentrated upon some mental creative process.

To apply the principle of self-mastery to the moral nature, the true method is, not to say no to the wrong, but to say yes to the right.

To control yourself in the midst of temptation, divert your attention from those things that you do not want, and cause the will to act upon the inner consciousness of those qualities and virtues that you do want.

To resist temptation is to fix attention upon the very thing that you do not wish to do; the mind will think more and more of the wrong until it becomes oblivious to the right, and will consequently do what it was tempted to do.

To concentrate the whole of attention upon the wrong is to cause all the tendencies of mind to move towards the wrong; the mind will think the wrong and be placed in bondage to the wrong; it will follow the wrong and act accordingly.

The secret of overcoming temptation is to refuse to give the wrong step a single moment of attention; do not resist it; do not even think about it, but give the whole of attention to the right step.

This will not be difficult if the mind, when concentrating upon the right step, will look within and view the superior side of the right step; because when its superiority is discerned, the interest in the right step will become so great that nothing could persuade the mind to think of anything else.

The various mental states of depression, gloom, despondency, worry, etc., are produced by the mind coming down to inferior planes of action. To control those states, that is, to remove them completely, turn all the forces of mind upon the highest state of consciousness that the imagination can picture. Then direct the will to act upon the finer consciousness of this state, and into the finer state the entire mind will go.

No attempt should be made to control the temper; this will simply place the mind more completely in bondage to the forces of temper. It will also give life and power to the present personal will.

When a person becomes angry he throws his thoughts out towards the object of his ill-will, thereby bringing consciousness to the surface, away from the real will and into the personal will. His energies are wasted, poise is lost, and practically all the actions of mind are misdirected; to try to control anything while in such a state would, therefore, be useless.

To avoid becoming angry under every circumstance, do not permit the actions of the mind to move outwardly against anything when antagonized, but direct all the forces of mind inwardly at once. This will prevent the antagonistic attitude, and so long as there is no antagonistic attitude there will be no feeling of anger.

To prevent thoughts from going out when provocations appear, impress daily upon mind the most perfect conception of a wholesome nature that can be formed, and train all the tendencies of mind to focus upon this ideal.

This will not only cause the creative energies of mind to build a sweet and wholesome nature, but the tendency of all feelings and emotions to move towards this inner ideal will become so strong that nothing can cause the force of feeling to go out against anything.

When this state has been established, all temper has been mastered, because all those forces that were previously wasted in temper have been turned in their courses, and are now engaged in the development of kindness, sympathy, tenderness and love.

To master anything is to turn it to better use; and all things are turned to better use that are trained to work in harmony with the law of continuous advancement.

To control circumstances, the principle is to establish in yourself what you wish your circumstances to be. The mind that has created the ideal mental world will gravitate, through absolute law, into an ideal physical world.

However, before man can create an ideal internal world he must attain that state of self-possession where he will not be influenced by the adverse in the external world. He must control himself in the midst of circumstances before circumstances will respond to his control.

In the midst of adverse circumstances, it is your thought and feeling that must be controlled, and to control thought under such circumstances all thought must be given to the ideal circumstance that you have in view.

To meet and overcome adversity it must be approached, not as an enemy, but as a force that can be turned to a better use. Adversity is but misdirected energy; but if you remain calm and strong, it will follow you, and do what you may desire to have done.

When you become stronger in your own conscious being than the forces that are about you, those forces will obey your will. For this reason, he who has mastered himself has mastered the universe.

The forces about you will not obey your will when you try to control them; they will follow you and obey you only when you have become stronger than they.

Circumstances do not have to be controlled; when the forces that are active in our circumstances are used intelligently, which means constructively, those circumstances will be in our hands without our trying to place them there.

It is necessary, however, to be calm and self-possessed in order to use those forces intelligently; therefore, the principal essential in the midst of circumstances is to control the mode of thinking. He who can do this can turn everything to good account that may enter his path.

There is only one mode of thinking that is conducive to self-mastery and that is scientific thinking; therefore, to control thinking is to think scientifically.

To think scientifically is to cause all the forces of mind to work together for the object that one has in view; and when all the forces of mind work for this object, the forces of circumstance will work for the same object; that is, if the force of mind is stronger than the force of circumstance.

Every person that thinks scientifically, and that unites all his forces upon the one object in view, will be stronger than his circumstances, and will thereby control those circumstances absolutely.

In the last analysis therefore the control of everything depends upon the control of self, and must necessarily follow the control of self; but he who would control himself must not try to control himself; he must not try to control anything; in brief, he must eliminate completely every desire that desires to exercise the power to rule. Instead, he must place himself absolutely in the consciousness of that power within that does rule—the power that is supreme.

He who gives himself to supreme power, will give expression to his own supreme power; and the expression of supreme power through every part of the self constitutes the mastery of self.

# The Masterpieces
## beautiful gift volumes

## The Progress Series

# Mastery of Fate

BY

## CHRISTIAN D. LARSON

*Author of*

HOW TO STAY YOUNG
THE IDEAL MADE REAL
THE PATHWAY OF ROSES
YOUR FORCES AND HOW TO USE THEM

———

L. N. FOWLER & CO.
7, Imperial Arcade, Ludgate Circus
LONDON, E. C.

1910
THE PROGRESS COMPANY
CHICAGO

# MASTERY OF FATE

# Mastery of Fate

WHAT man is, and what man does, determines in what conditions, circumstances and environments he shall be placed. And since man can change both himself and his actions, he can determine what his fate is to be.

To change himself, man must change his thought, because man is as he thinks; and to change his actions, he must change the purpose of his life, because every action is consciously or unconsciously inspired by the purpose held in view.

To change his thought, man must be able to determine what impressions are to form in his mind, because every thought is created in the likeness of a mental impression.

To choose his own mental impressions, man must learn to govern the objective senses, and must acquire the art of original thought.

Everything that enters the mind through the physical senses will produce impressions upon the mind, unless prevented by original thought. These impressions will be direct reflections of the environment from whence they came; and since thoughts will be created in the exact likeness of these impressions, so long as man permits environment to impress the mind, his thoughts will be exactly like his environment; and since man becomes like the thoughts he thinks, he will also become like his environment.

But man, in this way, not only grows into the likeness of his environment, but is, in addition, controlled by his environment, because his thoughts, desires, motives and actions are suggested to him by the impressions that he willingly accepts from environment.

Therefore, one of the first essentials in the mastery of fate is to learn to govern the physical senses so thoroughly, that no impression can enter mind from without, unless it is consciously desired.

This is accomplished by holding the mind in a strong, firm, positive attitude at all times, but especially while surrounded by conditions that are inferior.

This attitude will bring the senses under the supremacy of the subconscious will, and will finally produce a state of mind that never responds to impressions from without unless directed to do so.

To overcome the tendency of the physical senses to accept, indiscriminately, all sorts of impressions from without, mind should, at frequent intervals, employ the physical senses in trying to detect the superior possibilities that may be latent in the various surrounding conditions. And gradually, the senses themselves will become selective, and will instantaneously inform the mind whenever an undesirable impression demands admission.

While the senses are being employed in the search of superior possibilities, the impressions thus received should be analyzed, and re-combined in the constructive states of consciousness, and according to the mind's own original conception. This will promote original thinking, which will, in turn, counteract the tendency of the objective side of mind to receive suggestions from without.

Every original thought that mind may create, will to a degree, change man and re-make him according to what he inwardly desires to be; because every original thought is patterned after man's conception of himself when he is at his best.

Thoughts inspired by environment are inferior or superior, according to what the environment may be; but an original thought is always superior, because it is inspired by man himself while the superior elements of his being are predominant.

When every thought that mind creates is an original thought, man will constantly grow in greatness, superiority and worth; and when all these original thoughts are created with the same purpose in view, man will become exactly what is indicated by that purpose.

Therefore, since man can base thinking upon any purpose that he may desire, he can, through original thinking, become whatever he may choose to become.

Fate is the result of man's being and doing; a direct effect of the life and the works of the individual; a natural creation of man; and the creation is always the image and likeness of the creator.

Therefore, when man, through original thinking, acquires the power to become what he chooses to become, his fate will of itself change as man changes; and through this law he can create for himself any fate desired.

That man will consciously and naturally create his own fate when he gains the power to re-create himself as he desires to be, is evident for various reasons. And the power to re-create himself is simply the power of original thought. Because man becomes like the thoughts he thinks, and original thoughts are created in the likeness of man's ideal impressions of his superior self.

That the fate of each individual person is the direct, or indirect result of what that person is and does, can be demonstrated by the following self-evident facts:

The mental world in which a person lives is the exact reflection of what that person is, feels and thinks; therefore, when a superior life and worthier thoughts are attained, the mental world will also change accordingly.

The circumstances and conditions of man's physical world are the direct or indirect effects of the active elements in his mental world; a fact we shall thoroughly demonstrate in the following pages.

Like attracts like; therefore, the associations of man are after his own kind; and as he changes for the better he will attract, and be attracted into better associations.

The events that transpire in the life of man are the consequences of his own efforts to express himself in his individual world of action. Therefore, what happens to any person is the reaction of what that person has previously said or done.

This being true, man has the power to cause any event to transpire that he may decide upon; though to accomplish this it is necessary to understand the law of action and reaction as applied both to the physical and metaphysical worlds.

When man begins to re-create himself, he will rise superior to his present position; and since new and better opportunities always appear when man proves himself superior to his present position, he can, by changing himself as he desires, call forth any opportunity that he may desire.

To have the privilege to take advantage of better opportunities, is the direct path to better conditions, better circumstances and better environments; and since man can create this privilege at will, he can create his own fate, his own future, his own destiny.

However, the secret of creating this privilege at will, lies in man's power to form only such impressions upon his mind as will originate constructive thought. Because when all the thought he thinks is constructive, every mental process will be a building process, and will constantly increase the ability, the capacity and the personal worth of man himself. This in turn makes man competent to accept the larger places that are waiting everywhere for minds with sufficient capability to fill them.

Every thought has creative power; and this power will express itself according to the desire that was in mind when the thought was created. Therefore, if every thought is to express its creative power in the building up of man, mind must constantly be filled with the spirit of that purpose.

When the desire for growth and superior attainment does not predominate in mind, the greater part of the creative energy of thought will misdirect, and artificial mental conditions will form, only to act as obstacles to man's welfare and advancement.

The creative power of thought is the only power employed in the construction and reconstruction of man; and for this reason man is as he thinks.

Consequently, when man thinks what he desires to think, he will become what he desires to become. But to think what he desires to think, he must consciously govern the process through which impressions are formed upon mind.

To govern this process is to have the power to exclude any impression from without that is not desired, and to completely impress upon mind every original thought that may be formed; thus giving mind the power to think only what it consciously chooses to think.

Before man can govern this process, he must understand the difference between the two leading attitudes of mind—the attitude of self-submission, and the attitude of self-supremacy; and must learn how to completely eliminate the former, and how to establish all life, all thought, and all action absolutely upon the latter.

When this is done, no impression can form upon mind without man's conscious permission; and complete control of the creative power of thought is permanently secured.

To master the creative power of thought is to master the personal self; and to master the personal self is to master fate.

MAN is inherently master over everything in his own life, because the principle of his being contains the possibility of complete mastership; and the realization of this principle produces the attitude of self-supremacy.

While mind is in this attitude, only those impressions are formed that are consciously selected; consequently, only those thoughts are created that conform to the purpose which may predominate in mind at the time.

To remain constantly in the attitude of self-supremacy, is therefore the secret of original thinking; and since the mastery of fate comes directly from original thinking, everything that interferes with the attitude of self-supremacy must be eliminated completely.

The most serious obstacle to this attitude is the belief that man is, for the greater part, the product of his environment; and that man cannot change to any extent until a change is first produced in his environment.

The result of this belief is the attitude of self-submission; and the more deeply this belief is felt, the more completely does man submit himself to the influence of his surroundings.

While mind is in this attitude, it has only a partial control over the process of thinking; it accepts willingly every impression that may enter through the senses, and permits the creation of thought in the likeness of those impressions without the slightest discrimination.

To remove the attitude of self-submission, man must cease to believe that he is controlled by environment, and must establish all his thinking upon the conviction that he is inherently master over his entire domain.

This, however, may appear to be not only impossible, but absurd, when considered in the presence of the fact that man is controlled by environment. To tell a man to cease to believe as true that which he knows to be true, may not, at first sight seem to contain any reason; but at second sight it proves itself to mean the same as to tell a man to leave the darkness and enter the light.

When man ceases to believe that he is controlled by environment, he departs from a belief that is detrimental; and when he begins to realize that he has the power to completely control himself, he enters a conviction that is favorable to the highest degree.

While he is in the attitude of self-submission, he is controlled by environment, and the belief that he is thus controlled, is true to him. But when he enters the attitude of self-supremacy, he is not controlled by environment; therefore, the belief that he is controlled by environment is no longer true to him.

While we are in the dark, we can truthfully say that we are in darkness; but when we enter the light, we cannot say, truthfully, that we are in darkness.

There is such a thing as being influenced by conditions that exist in our surroundings; but when we transcend that influence we are in it no more; therefore, to say that we are in it when we are out of it, is to contradict ourselves. And we equally contradict ourselves when we state that we are controlled by environment after we are convinced that we are inherently masters of everything in the personal life.

What is not true to us now, we should not admit now, even though it had been true to us for all previous time.

To state that you are controlled by environment, and to permit that belief to possess your mind, is to submit yourself almost completely to the control of environment.

To recognize the principle of your being, and to realize that within that principle the power of complete supremacy does exist; to establish yourself absolutely upon that principle, and to state that you are not controlled by environment, is to depart from the control of environment.

While you are conscious of the principle of self-supremacy, you are unconscious of the influence of environment; therefore, to speak the truth, you must declare that you are complete master in your own domain.

When you know that the possibility of self-supremacy is within you, you can not state truthfully that it is not there; and to state, in the presence of your knowledge of self-supremacy, that you are controlled by environment, is the same as to state that there is no self-supremacy.

The very moment that you admit the possibility of self-supremacy, the control of environment is no longer a real fact to you; because in the state of self-supremacy, it is not possible for the control of environment to exist.

When man discovers the state of self-supremacy, he can no longer believe in the control of environment as a principle; and is therefore compelled to declare that the control of environment is no longer true to him. And, as he is permitted to speak only for himself, and judge only his own life, he must refuse absolutely to believe in the control of environment under any condition whatever.

To believe that others are controlled by environment, is to judge where he has no authority, and also to place himself once again in the belief that environment controls man. To place himself in that belief is to enter the attitude of self-submission, and submit himself to the influence of everything that enters his sphere of existence.

It is therefore evident that the principal reason why those who know of self-supremacy do not master fate, is because they are not true to their own convictions. They believe that the principle of self-supremacy exists, but they also believe that the control of environment exists. They try to believe both to be true at the same time, which is impossible.

If the one exists as a living power in the life of a person, the other does not exist in the life of that person. It would be just as reasonable to believe that light and darkness could exist in the same place at the same time.

To try to believe in the idea of self-supremacy and the control of environment at the same time, is to live in confusion; and he who lives in confusion controls practically nothing. He is therefore more or less controlled by everything.

When man is convinced that he is, in himself, master over his life, he can no longer believe that his life is controlled by environment. He must absolutely reject the latter belief; both can not be true to any one mind; therefore, every mind must decide which one of these beliefs to accept as absolutely true, and which one to reject as absolutely untrue.

The mind that does not wholly reject one of the two, is trying to serve two masters, which is impossible. He who tries to serve two masters will serve the one only, and that one will be the false one; because whoever tries to serve two masters is false to himself, and will consequently serve that which is false.

In this connection it may be questioned how we know that the principle of self-supremacy does exist; and how we know that complete mastership is inherent in man.

But we do know; because man does exercise complete mastership over certain parts of his being at certain times; and the fact that he does this proves the existence of the principle.

If the principle of self-supremacy did not exist, man could not exercise complete control over anything at any time; but every mind demonstrates supremacy many times every hour.

The mastership exercised over mind and body in various ways may be confined to limited spheres of action; but within those spheres of action the mastership is complete. And those spheres will expand constantly as the principle of self-supremacy is applied on a larger and a larger scale.

Since the principle of complete control exists in man, there is a way to apply that principle in everything, and at all times. But to accomplish this, the attitude of self-supremacy must prevail at all times, and under all conditions.

While man is in the attitude of self-supremacy, he exercises complete control over certain things in his life; but when he enters the belief that he is controlled or influenced by other things, he leaves the attitude of self-supremacy, and ceases to exercise his complete control.

In the present state of human development, the average mind is so constituted that it oscillates from one state to another, remaining the greater part of the time in the attitude of self-submission; due principally to the fact that we are seldom absolutely true to the higher conviction, and also because we try to think that both beliefs are true at the same time.

Consequently, the great essential for man in his present state is to accept the high conviction as an absolute truth, and be true to that truth every moment of existence.

To be true to that truth he must refuse absolutely to believe that he can be controlled or influenced by anything or anybody. He must depart completely from the belief in the control of other powers, and must recognize in himself the only power to control—the power to control completely, everything in his own domain.

Nor is this a contradiction, because when man enters the consciousness of self-supremacy, he can not submit his self to any outside influence; therefore, there are no outside influences in action in his life.

And when this is the case he can not believe in the existence of outside influences, as far as he is concerned. When nothing is trying to control him, he can not truthfully say that he is being controlled, nor even that he is liable to be controlled.

When man is in a state of self-supremacy, he is in a state where no influence from without exists; he is in a world where the power of self-mastery is the only controlling power; therefore, he can not truthfully recognize any other.

While in the attitude of self-submission, your mind is open to all kinds of impressions from without; and consequently, your thinking will be suggested to you by your environment. The result is that you will become like your environment, and will think, act and live as your environment may suggest.

If your environment be inferior, you will think inferior thoughts, live an inferior life, and commit deeds that are low or perverse, so long as you are in the attitude of self-submission. But if you should submit yourself to a better environment, your life, thoughts, and deeds would naturally become better. In each case you would be the representation of the impressions that enter through the senses.

However, the very moment you pass from a superior environment to one that is inferior, you will begin to change for the worse, unless you have in the meantime attained a degree of self-supremacy.

To enter a superior environment will not of itself develop self-supremacy, nor the art of original thinking; because so long as you permit yourself to be influenced by environment, you prevent your mind from gaining consciousness of the principle of self-supremacy.

A change of environment, therefore, will not give man the power to master his fate. This power comes only through a change of thought.

While in the attitude of self-supremacy your mind is not open to impressions from any source; but you can place your mind, at will, in the responsive attitude, so that it may receive impressions from any source that you may select.

By proper selection, consciousness can, in this way, be trained to express itself only through those mental channels that reach the superior side of things, and thereby come in contact with the unlimited possibilities of things.

From impressions received through this contact with unlimited possibilities, mind will be able to form original thoughts that embody superior powers and attainments; and as man becomes like his thoughts, he will, through this process, become superior.

Instead of being controlled by the impressions received from environment, he will control those impressions, and use them as material in the construction of his own larger life, and the greater destiny that must follow.

While mind is in the attitude of self-supremacy, man's contact with the world will not affect him contrary to the way he desires to be affected; because he controls the impressions that come from without, and can completely change their natures before they are accepted in consciousness. Or, he may refuse to accept them entirely.

In the midst of adversity he does not permit the adverseness of the circumstances to impress his mind, but opens his mind to be impressed by the great power that is back of the adversity. His mind is not impressed by the misdirection of power, but by the power itself.

Therefore, instead of being disturbed, he is made stronger.

There is something of value to be gained from every disagreeable condition, because within every condition there is power, and there are always greater possibilities latent than the surface indicates.

Through original thinking these greater possibilities are discerned; and when mind is in the attitude of self-supremacy, it may choose to be impressed by the greater possibilities only, thus providing more material for the reconstruction of man, and his destiny, on a larger and superior scale.

It is therefore evident that self-supremacy is indispensable; and it is attained by placing all life, all thought and all action upon the principle that man is inherently master over everything in his life; and by refusing absolutely to believe that we can be controlled by environment under any condition whatever.

THE statement that the conditions and circumstances of man's physical world are the direct, or indirect effects of the active elements in his mental world, is fully demonstrated by comparing the external and internal phases of life in any person. The correspondence between the two is exact.

Every misfortune in the life of any individual, barring accidents produced by nature, can be traced to incompetence in some way, or to the misapplication of ability. And even those adverse conditions that come from nature's seeming irregularities can be wholly avoided through the development of superior insight.

The largest number of misfortunes comes from doing the wrong thing at the wrong time; and this is caused by confusion in the mental world, or by an obtuse judgment.

The mind that is constantly in a state of poise and harmony, judges well, and will never misdirect any thought, force or action. Therefore, by cultivating those states, anyone can gain the power to do the right thing at the right time.

A great many conditions that surround

the average individual are not produced by himself, and for this reason he does not hold himself responsible; but when a person enters circumstances that have been created by others, he simply enters something that corresponds with his own mental world.

No person with normal mind will voluntarily enter conditions that are inferior, or that do not correspond in any way to himself. The fact that he accepts, or borrows the environments produced by others, proves that he either belongs there, or that he does not know where he belongs.

When we enter blindly into disagreeable circumstances, our own blindness is at fault; therefore, the external circumstance is the indirect effect of a certain action in our own minds.

A person with great ability, who can practically apply his ability, will never be found at work where recompense is inadequate. Though a person with great ability who does not possess the practical element, may remain in a position that is inferior. In this case ability is misdirected, and the person's own mentality is the indirect cause of the undesirable circumstance.

The mind that is gentle, orderly and beautiful in character will inspire admiration in many places where associations are exactly to his liking. He is wanted among the best of his kind, and has the privilege to select the characters of his social world. Others may call him fortunate, but he has attracted ideal associations because he himself can give ideal companionship. Having developed a worthy mind, he belongs where minds of worth congregate; and through such associations gains inspiration for the development of still greater worth. This not only promotes his advancement in his field of action, but enables him to attract, meet and enjoy still better associations in the future.

When a beautiful character is found among inferior associations, the cause is usually a lack of positive quality. A number of beautiful characters are purely negative, and are therefore hiding the greater part of their true worth. They are far better than they appear to be, and they possess more than they use; but as it is only what we use that counts, such characters will be found in associations that measure exactly, not with what they are, but with what they use and express.

A genius may have no opportunity to employ his great ability; and if so, there is a reason. If he is really competent, there are a hundred excellent places open to him; but if he has only genius and little or no talent, he is not competent. If he has only the capacity, but not the art of turning his power to practical use, he can do nothing of value; and it is results that merit the good places in life.

His misfortune is therefore not due to any exterior adversity, but is caused directly by a state of his own mind.

His misfortune, however, will vanish, and great and good things come instead, when he transforms his genius into talent, and learns to do something that the world wants done.

There is many a skilled workman who keeps himself down because he is constantly out of harmony with his associations. By resisting everything and antagonizing everybody, he keeps his own inferior side always in view. His skill is submerged beneath his personal inferiority, and he is judged, not by what he hides, but by the imperfections that he willingly presents to the world.

A man who persists in revealing nothing but his inferior side, can not expect promotion; to promote such a man would be a loss to the institution; and those in authority usually feel this fact instinctively.

Every enterprise is continued for results; therefore, everything that interferes with results should be eliminated. To give a conspicuous place to some one who breeds discord, hatred and confusion, will positively interfere with results; therefore, such a person does not justly deserve promotion, no matter how perfect his individual product may be.

The man who is against the world will array the world against himself, and must take the consequences. His fate will not be pleasant, but he alone is to blame.

To do good work is necessary; but it is also necessary to make good as a man, if the best places are to be secured. Therefore, hide your inferior side until you have destroyed it entirely. Surround your skillful labor with a personal atmosphere that breeds harmony, wholesomeness and character, and the best position in your field of action will be opened to you.

There are thousands of people who claim they have not secured a fair chance; but if that be true, the mental worlds of those very persons are the causes. There is something in their mental make-up that places their ability and skill in a false light before the world.

The same is true of the man who is constantly misunderstood. He is not revealing himself as he really is; his real nature is misdirected during the process of expression, and everybody is deceived. That something that produces the deception exists in the person's own mind, and so long as that something remains, he will misplace himself, and will not meet the friends nor the opportunities that really are his own.

The misplacing of oneself is due to a lack of judgment, or to a mal-arrangement of one's personal powers and characteristics.

But judgment can be remarkably improved in anyone through the development of original thinking and interior insight; and the various powers of the person can be placed in perfect order and harmony with each other through the practice of bringing out the greater possibilities in every phase of being.

The habit of permitting everything we come in contact with to impress our minds, and suggest this course or that method is responsible for a great deal of misdirected effort; therefore, the attitude of self-supremacy becomes indispensable.

A large number of people have been induced to enter circumstances where they do not belong, through the exercise of an abnormal sympathy. Such a sympathy, called forth by a few selfish friends, has also kept many a great mind working in a narrow field, while scores of large, and even extraordinary opportunities were constantly waiting.

To correct this condition, train yourself to sympathize only with the superior side of people and the greater possibilities of things.

When you sympathize naturally and constantly with the superior side of people, all the desires of mind will gradually fix their attention upon the superior; and when all the desires of mind desire the superior you will be irresistably drawn into superior association. And nothing, not even old abnormal sympathies can keep you away from your own.

When you sympathize with the greater possibilities in things, your attention will be constantly turned upon the greater; your mind will be more and more impressed with the greater, until every thought becomes a power for greatness; and with this power you will move into greatness, regardless of any obstacle that may appear in the way.

The power of sympathy is one of the greatest powers of attraction in existence; therefore, when we sympathize only with the superior, we will be drawn into superiority, and this will steadily change our environments for the better. Thus, by producing a change in the mental world, we can revolutionize the external world.

When life is viewed comprehensively, it becomes very evident that the actions of the person determine what the external conditions and circumstances of that person are to be; but every personal action is caused by a mental action; therefore, the change of environment must be preceded by a change of mind.

To master thought is to master fate; but thought can not be mastered until mind acts exclusively upon the principle that man is inherently complete master over his entire domain.

The strongest evidence that can be produced in favor of the statement that man's circumstances are caused by the active elements of his mental world, is that of creative ability, because it is being demonstrated every day that the man with a strong creative mind has destiny at his feet.

Creative ability can absolutely change all circumstances; but it is not an external power; it is simply an active element in mind.

THE mastery of fate implies the constant improvement of everything in one's world—physical or mental; and since the improvement of one's exterior environment requires financial increase, the problem of recompense and reward must be solved.

There are vast numbers who claim they are not being remunerated according to their worth, and this claim is keeping the industrial world in constant turmoil.

The result is detrimental to everybody, whether they are directly connected with industrial activity or not. Therefore, to find a solution for the problem would be one of the greatest discoveries that could possibly be made.

That a great deal of injustice exists in the world, is true; and that many who are strong are taking advantage of multitudes that are weak, is also true; but there is a peaceful way for every individual to secure his own. And it remains wholly with the individual.

There is no remedy in sight that the whole world can adopt, through which industrial justice can be established by law; but each individual can so relate himself to the world that his recompense will correspond exactly with his worth.

To do this he must neither under-value nor over-value his work; and he must not compare his legitimate efforts with the efforts of those who employ questionable means.

There are a great many who think they are worth more than they really are, because they compare themselves with the unscrupulous.

When a certain person gains great wealth through illegitimate means, many imagine that they ought to gain as much; they are just as good and just as able as he, and work equally as hard.

But in the mastery of fate all kinds of unjust methods must be eliminated completely, because in the creation of one's future there must be no flaws, or the entire structure may have to be discarded.

There is no wisdom in making any comparison between oneself and the man who is gaining wealth by undermining his own future welfare. We do not care for the destiny of such a personage, and there is only loss in store for those who imitate his ways.

Whether we are gaining as much as this one or that one is not the question at all; the question is, are we receiving what we are actually worth? If we are not, we must find the cause, and the way to remove that cause.

If you are receiving all that you deserve, make yourself more deserving, and you will receive more; but if you are not receiving your share, learn the reason why. If you are to blame, change yourself; if your present work is to blame, use your present work as a stepping stone to something better.

The average person who thinks he is underpaid, will find himself to be the real cause; therefore, the change of himself is the remedy. And he is usually to blame in this respect, that he overvalues his work and undervalues himself.

No one can advance in life unless he values himself correctly. The man who lives a "common" life, and continues in "ordinary" attitudes of mind will stay "down," no matter how hard he works or how well he performs his particular labor. For this there are several reasons.

It is not simply the visible product of brains or skill that the world pays for; the world also pays for what man contributes to life.

If your personal life is inferior, you give your vocation the stamp of inferiority; and a "common" atmosphere, so detrimental to the progress of any enterprise, goes with you, wherever you may be employed.

If you carry an atmosphere of worth, advancement is in store without fail, because the world does recognize worth, and pays well to secure it.

It is not only the work, but the life that surrounds that work that counts. It is not only the idea, but the words through which it is expressed that carry conviction. And it is not only the ability of the man, but the way he presents that ability that commands attention from the world.

When you present your ability in a crude, common attitude, and present yourself in an atmosphere of inferiority, you are hiding the larger part of your worth, your ability and your skill. And you will be paid only for that which the world can see.

The rays of a skilled mind or a brilliant intellect can not be seen at first sight, through the dense atmosphere of personal recklessness and crudeness; and the world does not possess the second sight.

But no man can surround himself with a clear atmosphere—an atmosphere that reveals the best there is in him—unless he values himself, and aims to express his real worth in every thought and action.

If a man has superior ability, let him demonstrate by his own presence that he is neither common, inferior nor ordinary. The world demands demonstration; and any one can detect a real man, no matter what clothes he may wear.

The world is constantly in search of competent men, and when you prove yourself to be competent, you will have more rare opportunities than you can fill.

When the average man begins to live, and takes just as much pride in living a real life as he does in producing a good machine, the industrial world will be revolutionized for the better, and every man will receive all that he knows he is worth.

To value yourself correctly, understand the unbounded possibilities that are latent within you, and live in the realization of the greater things which you know you have the power to do. This will produce in mind the consciousness of superiority, and through this consciousness, superior impressions will be formed in mind. From these impressions will come superior thoughts; which in turn will develop superiority in you; because a man is as he thinks.

The principal reason why a man who is down, remains there, and continues to appear as ordinary as his environment, is because he permits his mind to be impressed with everything that his environment may suggest. His thoughts are therefore the reflections of his surroundings, and he is like his thoughts.

Therefore, the man who would become different from his environment must learn the art of original thinking, and must enter the attitude of self-supremacy.

The principal reason why a man is underpaid is because he does not value himself, and therefore hides behind personal inferiority the greater part of his ability.

Another reason is because he works only for the wages that are coming to himself. He refuses to do more than is absolutely necessary, lest some one might be benefited. This attitude produces the cramped condition, which in turn reacts upon the purse.

The man who is afraid to do too much, usually fails to do enough; at any rate, he produces that impression, and his recompense is lowered accordingly.

On the other hand, the man who does his best at all times, regardless of the scale of wages, not only produces an excellent impression everywhere, but makes those in authority feel that he wants the enterprise to succeed. He is therefore better paid, because such men are valuable. They are wanted everywhere, not because they do more than they are paid for, but because they are a living power for success wherever they are called upon to act.

The spirit of success breeds success;

and the man who takes a living interest in the enterprise for which he works, even doing more than he is expected to do when the occasion demands, is creating the spirit of success, and will soon share in the greater success that follows.

Among the underpaid, by far the largest number is composed of those who submit absolutely to their present conditions, and therefore remain not only in bondage to unscrupulous task-masters, but also to their own environments and mental limitations.

They are the many weak, of whom some of the strong take advantage; and it is in behalf of these that reformers demand a change in the order of things. But it is not a change in the order of things that the world requires; it is a *change of mind.* And when the change of mind is produced, all other necessary changes will inevitably follow.

If you are underpaid because you have submitted to the power of the unscrupulous, cease to live in the attitude of mental submission. Do not antagonize the powers to which you have submitted, and do not resist your present condition. In your external life continue as usual for a period; but change absolutely your internal life.

What we resist we fear; and we always continue in bondage to that which we fear.

What we antagonize, we meet on the inferior side, and thus enter into contact with the very things we desire to avoid. We shall never get rid of the inferior so long as we resist the inferior; and whatever stays with us will impress our minds. Therefore, by resisting the inferior, we produce inferiority in ourselves.

Begin your emancipation by removing your attitude of self-submission; cease to believe that you must remain down where you are. Change your mind; know that inherently you are master over everything in your own domain, and resolve to exercise your supremacy. Refuse to be impressed by your environment; and learn to impress your own mind with superior impressions only. Re-create your own mind according to a higher standard of power, ability and character; thus you will re-create both yourself and your surroundings; because by making yourself stronger and more competent, you will be wanted where surroundings are better, and recompense greater.

The reason why those who are mentally weak remain in submission to inferior environments, is because they either do not attempt to become strong, or because they use up their mental powers resisting adversity.

Every person, no matter how submerged

he may be, who will arouse his own interior strength, exercise his own supremacy over his thoughts, thus thinking his own superior thought, will gradually rise out of his condition; and ere long he will find both emancipation and the reward of a better place in life.

This is the only orderly method to freedom; and will produce permanent freedom. And it is the only natural method to greater gain and better conditions.

However, attention must not be centered too much upon mere financial gain. The principle is abundance of everything that is necessary to produce a complete life on all conscious planes; and the perpetual increase of all these things as life eternally advances.

But these things man himself must create; and creative power increases through the development of character, ability and self-supremacy.

O master fate it is necessary to approach all the elements of fate in the proper mental attitudes; because since everything in the external world responds to the active forces in one's mental world, these forces should so act as to call forth only the response desired.

The idea of mastery will arouse in the average mind a tendency to control objective things with the will; but we must remember that fate is not controlled; fate is created.

When we can create any fate that we may desire, we have mastered fate; but not until then.

The mastery of fate does not call for the controlling actions of the will, but for the constructive actions of the creative energies; and since the domineering use of the will scatters creative energy, such an attitude of mind must never be permitted.

All desire to control or influence persons or things must be eliminated completely, because such a course will only defeat our purpose.

We do not master fate by compelling things to come our way; or by persuading persons to promote our objects in view.

Things will come of themselves when we demonstrate our ability to use things; and persons will co-operate with us in every way possible when we prove the superiority of both ourselves and our work.

The weakest mind of all is the domineering mind, and since such a mind has but little creative energy, the man who domineers can not fulfill, legitimately, a single desire. And what he does control through force, will later on react to his own downfall.

It is the meek that inherit the earth, because such minds have the greatest creative power. What we create, we inherit; no more, no less. Therefore, when we gain the power to create much, we shall inherit much.

To meet everything in the attitude of harmony is of the highest importance, because whatever we enter into harmony with, while in a state of aspiration, that we meet on the superior side.

The qualities that we enter into mental contact with, we absorb; therefore, it is a great advantage to mentally meet the superior only.

When we constantly aspire, and live in harmony with everything, we enter into true relationship with the better qualities that are latent in every person or condition with which we come in contact; and consequently permit the superior things in life to impress our minds at every turn. And the value of having only superior impressions in mind is so great that it can not be calculated.

Superior impressions originate superior thoughts; and as man is as he thinks, superior thoughts will develop superiority in him. And the superior man creates a superior fate, a better future and a more wonderful destiny.

By entering into harmony with all things, and by constantly dwelling in the aspiring attitude, you absorb the good qualities from your enemies and your adversaries. And since evil is only the good perverted, when you take the good out of anything, there is nothing left to be perverted; consequently there can exist no more enmity nor adversity in that place.

Absorb the good power that is back of adversity, and adversity ceases to be. In this way, we can truthfully say, "We have met the enemy, and they are ours," because the very life of that which was against us has been appropriated by ourselves and engaged to work for our interest and promotion.

This principle, if carried out in every detail of life, would completely revolutionize physical and mental existence; and would reduce trouble, discord, adversity and enmity to practically nothing.

The most disagreeable circumstances will change and become models of perfection simply through our attitude in calling forth the superior side; and when we enter into harmony with any circumstance while we are in the aspiring state of mind, we call forth the superior qualities of that circumstance, and the greater possibilities that are always latent everywhere.

When we meet circumstances of any description, we should never resist the undesirable elements, if there be any; nor find fault with the deficiency; but should search immediately for the possibilities. The questions are, what that circumstance can give; and how we may secure everything of worth that it can give.

Every circumstance you meet contains something for you; because it is made to enrich your life, to serve you, and to promote your welfare in every way possible.

By meeting a circumstance in the harmony of aspiration you call forth its real possibilities, and especially if you look directly for those possibilities. When you take an active interest and a friendly interest in the constructive powers of a circumstance, those powers will place themselves in your hands, and every disagreeable element will disappear.

By taking the best out of every circumstance, and by transmuting all the forces you meet so that they become your forces, you add so much to your present life that you rise readily to a higher position, where superior circumstances and still greater possibilities will be met.

Any circumstance can be changed, if constantly approached in this way; or you will change so much that far better circumstances will be ready to receive you.

Directly connected with the attitude of harmony is the attitude of love; and the way we love, as well as what we love, is of the highest importance in the mastery of fate.

The law is that we steadily grow into the likeness of that which we love; and the reason is that what we love is so deeply impressed upon mind that it never fails to reproduce itself in thought.

Anything that enters mind while mind is in the state of deep feeling, is deeply impressed; and it is the deepest impressions that serve as patterns for the creative energies.

Love only that which has high worth, and never permit the common, the ordinary or the inferior to enter the world of feeling.

Love the true side of life; love the soul-side of persons; and love the greater possibilities that are latent in circumstances, conditions and things. And love these things with a passion that thrills every atom in your being. The result will be simply remarkable.

Where the heart is, there we concentrate; and where we concentrate we give our life, our thought, our ability and our power. Therefore, if we wish to build up the superior, we must deeply love the high, the true and the worthy, wherever these may be found.

When difficulties are met, they should be met in the attitude of joy; and we should look upon the experience as a privilege through which greater power may be brought into evidence.

To count everything joy is not a mere sentiment, but the application of a great scientific principle.

The mind that meets everything in joy, conquers every time, because the attitude of joy is an ascending attitude; it transcends, and goes above that with which it comes in contact.

Therefore, whatever we meet in the attitude of joy, we rise above; and whatever we rise above, that we overcome in every instance.

The feeling of joy is also expansive, enlarging and constructive, and is a developing power of extreme value.

To count everything joy may at first seem difficult; but when we realize that the attitude of real joy rises above everything, and overcomes everything by taking life to a higher level, we shall soon find it easier and more natural to meet everything in joy than otherwise.

GREAT many new ideas of extreme value have recently appeared in current thought, but one of the most valuable is the idea that "he can who thinks he can;" and in the mastery of fate it will not only be necessary to keep this idea constantly in mind, but also to make the fullest possible use of the law upon which this idea is based.

To accomplish anything, ability is required; and it has been demonstrated that when man thinks he can do a certain thing, he increases the power and the capacity of that faculty which is required in doing what he thinks he can do.

To illustrate: When you think that you can succeed in business, you cause your business ability to develop, because by thinking that you can succeed in business you draw all the creative energies of the system into the business faculties, and consequently those faculties will be developed; and as those faculties are being developed, you gain that ability which positively can produce success in business.

You develop the power to do certain things by constantly thinking that you can do those things, because the law is that wherever in mind we concentrate attention, there development will take place; and we naturally concentrate upon that faculty that is required in the doing of that which we think we can do.

If you think that you can compose music, and continue to think that you can, you will develop that musical faculty that can compose music. Even though you may not have the slightest talent in that direction now, by thinking constantly that you can compose music you will develop that talent.

Results may begin to appear in a few months, or it may require a few years; nevertheless, if you continue to think that you can compose music, you will, in a few years be able to do so. Later on, you can develop into a rare musical genius.

Persistence, however, is required, and all thought must be concentrated daily upon that one accomplishment. But this will not be difficult, because ere long the entire mind will form a tendency to accumulate all its power and creative energy in the region of that one faculty; and constant development will take place both consciously and unconsciously.

Whatever a man desires to do, if he thinks that he can, he will develop the necessary power; and when the necessary power and ability are gained, the tangible results inevitably follow.

This law enables man to accomplish anything that he may desire. Whether a few weeks, a few years, or a life-time be required in reaching the goal, he positively will sooner or later reach the goal if he continues to *think* that he can.

Thought is creative; thought makes man what he is; and thought can change man or any of his mental qualities, if he chooses to have such changes made.

All desirable changes are due to greater development; and since thought is creative and does develop, wherever the creative power of thought is concentrated, there development will take place.

There are many ways to develop the various mental faculties through the concentration of thought, but the most penetrating and the most thorough method is to persistently and continually think that you can do what the faculty you wish to develop is created to do.

If you wish to become a great orator, continue to think that you can deliver a matchless oration; and if you persist in this process of thinking, your oratorical faculties will receive so much constructive thought, so much creative energy and so much power that a high development must positively take place in those faculties. The whole of mind will be given to oratory, and oratory can not fail to develop.

Whenever we give the whole of mind to any faculty, that faculty becomes remarkable; therefore, man can make himself remarkable in any direction he may choose.

The secret is persistence. After you have decided what you want to do, begin to think that you can, and continue without ceasing to think that you can. Pay no attention to temporary failures; know that you can, and continue to think that you can.

To continue in the consciousness of the law that underlies this idea will bring greater results and more rapid results, because in that case you will consciously direct the developing process, and you will know that to think you can is to develop the power that can.

To keep constantly before mind the idea that "he can who thinks he can," will steadily increase the qualities of faith, self-confidence, perseverance and persistence; and whoever develops these qualities to a greater and greater degree will move forward without fail.

Therefore, to live in the conviction that "he can who thinks he can," will not only increase ability along the desired lines, but will also produce the power to push that ability into a living, tangible action.

In addition to thinking that you can do, try to do; put into practice at once what power and ability you possess, and by continuing to think that you can do more, you will develop the power to do more.

To keep before mind the idea that "he can who thinks he can" will also hold attention upon the high ideals we have in view, and this is extremely important.

The fact is, if we do not give ideal models to the creative energies of mind, those energies will employ whatever passes before them, as the senses admit all sorts of impressions from without.

The creative energies of mind are constantly producing thought, and these thoughts will be produced in the likeness of the deepest, the clearest and the most predominant mental impressions. Therefore, it is absolutely necessary that the predominant impressions be those into the likeness of which we desire to grow, because, as the impressions are, so are the thoughts; and as the thoughts are, so is man.

When man thinks that he will succeed, the predominant impression is the idea of success. All his thoughts will therefore contain the elements of success, and the forces that can produce success; and he himself, will become thoroughly saturated with the very life of success.

Nothing succeeds like success; therefore, the man that is filled with the spirit of success can never fail; and what is more, the forces that contain the elements of success will give that man the very qualifications that are essential to success, because like produces like.

And again, the faculty required to produce the success desired, will be the one upon which all these success-energies will be concentrated.

When a man has the ability to do certain things, those things will be done; that is a foregone conclusion; and the ability to do what we want to do, comes when we constantly and persistently think that we can do what we want to do.

In the mastery of fate, the law upon which this idea is based will be found indispensable; because, since fate is created, and not controlled, all the elements of fate will have to be constantly re-created.

But no one can do this unless he thinks he can. To change many of the circumstances and conditions that now may surround us, requires more ability and power than we now possess; and to secure this greater power we must proceed to change and improve everything in our world by working in the conviction that we can.

By constantly thinking that we can

change all our conditions, we gain the power to produce that change, and will consequently reach our goal.

The man who faces his environment with the belief that he is helpless before so many insurmountable obstacles, will remain where he is; but the man who thinks he can, will proceed to surmount everything, overcome everything, change everything and improve everything; and by constantly thinking he can, he will gain the power to do what he thinks he can do.

HE purpose of life is continuous advancement, and this necessitates the constant appropriation of the new, and the constant elimination of the old. To promote the first essential, a practical system of ideals is required; and to promote the second, we must master the art of letting go.

If we desire the new to be created, the creative process of mind must be supplied with new and better impressions. Should we fail to do this, the creative energies will employ the old ideas, or impressions that are suggested from without.

In the mastery of fate, one of the greatest essentials is to prevent environment from impressing the mind; and to prevent this, your mind should be filled with your own ideal impressions. But this is not possible to any satisfactory degree unless a definite system of idealism is adopted, because no impression will become strong and predominant unless it is given constant attention.

In this connection, the true use of the imagination becomes extremely important. Everything that we imagine we impress upon mind; therefore, through the imagination we can work ourselves into almost any condition or state of being. In meeting circumstances and events imagination can be made to serve a most valuable service, and thus become directly instrumental in changing environment and fate.

When adversity comes we usually try to find the silver lining; but when we fail to find this, discouragement follows, which in turn but intensifies the darkness and the trouble.

However, we can create a silver lining with the imagination that will serve the same purpose; because when we picture the better side of things, and keep mind steadily upon that picture, the better will impress itself upon the mind. The result is that our thoughts change for the better, and we improve with our thoughts; and the improvement of man means the improvement of his environment.

Any one who is in trouble can work himself out by creating in his imagination the silver lining of emancipation, and keeping the eye single upon that ideal picture.

Any one who wishes to change his fate can do so by imaging upon mind a different fate, and by keeping that image so constantly before mind that every thought becomes the likeness of the new fate.

The law is that the external world of man

changes when his mental world changes; and through the constructive use of the imagination the mental world can be changed in any way that we may desire.

When failure seems near, we should image success, refusing absolutely to think of the dark side. By imaging success, we impress upon mind the idea of success; thoughts will be created containing the elements of success, and from these thoughts we shall receive the power that can produce success.

Any threatening failure can be overcome and entirely averted by this simple process, providing we live and work as we think.

By training the imagination to serve the system of ideals that we may have adopted, we shall soon gain full control of the process that forms impressions upon mind; and when this is accomplished every high ideal, every great purpose and every superior quality that we have in mind will be so well impressed upon the mental creative process that perpetual growth into every desirable condition must positively take place.

But to promote this advancement, we must learn to let go completely of everything that has served its purpose, or that in any way interferes with the steady progress of the whole man.

To acquire the art of letting go is an accomplishment with few equals, and is easily attained by learning to act upon the subjective side of everything in our own systems.

It is the subjective side that holds; therefore, the subjective side alone can let go. The subjective contains the root of every thought, every desire, every tendency, every physical condition and every mental state that exists in the human system; it is the foundation of every thing in the personal man, and originates the cause of everything that takes place in the life of man.

Whatever we place in the hands of the subjective, the subjective will continue to hold until it is called upon to let go. Every cause that gains a foothold in the subjective will continue to produce its effects, until the subjective is directed to have it removed; and every impression that is formed upon the subjective will continue to act as a pattern for the creation of thought until a different impression is formed in its place. To know how to deal with the subjective is therefore one of the greatest essentials; and the reason why so few have the power to master their fate is because the conscious direction of the subjective is almost unknown.

Mind has two sides, the outer and the inner; or the objective and the subjective. The objective is the conscious mind; the subjective is the subconscious mind. The objective acts; the subjective reacts. The objective mind gives orders; the subjective carries them out. The objective selects the seed and places that seed in the subjective; and the subjective causes that seed to grow and bear fruit after its kind. Whatever the objective desires to have done, the subjective has the power to do, and will do, if properly directed; though it must be properly and consciously directed.

In the average mind the subjective is directed ignorantly and irregularly; sometimes for good, more frequently otherwise. Therefore, the results are as they are; uncertain, unsatisfactory and limited.

However, when we learn to direct the subjective consciously and with method, we shall be able to produce any result desired, at any time desired.

To direct the subjective, the will must be employed, as it must be in all forms of direction; and in the use of the will is where the real secret is found. The will must not act upon the external phase of any idea, desire or condition, but must *intentionally* act upon the internal side only.

When you move a muscle, the will acts upon the subjective side of that muscle. If the will should act upon the objective side, the muscle would become stiff, unable to move at all. Likewise, when the will acts upon the objective side of any idea, desire, tendency, habit, mental state or physical condition, no change whatever will take place. But the very moment that the will acts upon the subjective side of those things, they will begin to change according to the desire predominant in mind at the time.

Therefore whatever we wish to remove from the subjective, we should direct the will *intentionally* upon the subjective side of that which we desire to remove, and *desire deeply* to have that something removed.

It may require some training to master this process, but when the process is mastered, we can drop anything from mind instantaneously. Any idea, any habit, any desire, any state of discord or confusion, any diseased condition—all can be eliminated completely from the system, when we acquire the art of letting go.

To train the objective mind to act directly upon the subjective, consciousness should be more thoroughly developed in the realms of the finer feelings and the finer elements of life. Efforts should be made to come in touch with the higher vibrations *in* the system, because whenever we act in the higher vibrations, we act upon the subjective.

Whatever we desire the subjective to do while we act *in* the finer feeling of the higher vibrations, that the subjective will proceed to do.

To act consciously and directly upon the subjective will also deepen the realization of life, which is extremely important; because the deepest life gives the strongest power, and in the creation of a greater destiny we need all the power we can secure.

When this deepening of life is continued in the serene attitude, mind is kept constantly in touch with the source of unbounded power, and thus receives as much power each day as may be required.

This brings us to one of the greatest essentials in the mastery of fate—living; because there is nothing that contributes so much to the supremacy of man as a real, full life.

To bring out the best that is within him, man must not merely exist; he must live. When man actually lives he is what he is, and is all that he is. He does not try to be something else, or someone else. He does not imitate, but continues to be himself. And this is one of the secrets in the creation of a greater destiny.

The average person does not try to be himself, but tries constantly to imitate. He does not try to bring out his own individuality, but tries to fashion his personality and personal life according to some exterior model that is supposed to be the standard in the world's eye. The result is, he misplaces himself; because a person is always misplaced and misdirected when he tries to imitate the life of another; and no misplaced person can master his own fate.

Such a mind goes willingly and unconsciously into all sorts of foreign conditions, and then wonders what he has done to bring about such a mixed and undesirable fate.

When the individual tries to be himself, he will begin to act wholly in his own world, the only world where he can be his very best. And by trying to be himself, he begins to draw upon the unbounded possibilities that exist within himself, thus making himself a larger and a greater being constantly.

The individual that tries to imitate persons or environments does not express himself; therefore, his own hidden powers continue to lie dormant.

To express one's own individuality, and to be oneself, the greatest essential is to live real life; the life that is felt in the depth of inner consciousness.

To be yourself, be all that you are where you are, and greater spheres of action will constantly open before you. Be satisfied to be what you are, but do not be satisfied to be less than all that you are.

When one begins to live in the depth of

real life, and begins to draw upon his own
inexhaustible self, he will find that he is so
much that there is no end to the possibilities that exist in his own life and his own
world.

EVERY person finds himself in a certain environment, in a certain physical condition, in certain mental states, with certain abilities and opportunities, and with certain obstacles and limitations.

In a world with others, he finds himself in a world of his own; and he calls this world his fate. But what is the cause of it all?

He knows that he is responsible for some of it, but he is quite sure he is not responsible for all of it. But who is? He wishes to know, in order that he may eliminate the undesirable, and constantly improve upon that which he wishes to retain.

When we analyze fate we find that it has four distinct parts, each of which comes from its own individual cause.

The first is the creations of nature that man has voluntarily entered into; the second is the creations of the race that man as an individual has accepted as his own; the third is the creations of certain individuals to which man has closely related himself; and the fourth is the creations of the individual himself.

That man voluntarily entered into the

first three, is a fact easily demonstrated; though he might not have been wide awake when he did so. Those parts of your fate that you have not created, you have selected; though too often you made your selection in the dark.

In the mastery of fate it is therefore not only necessary to produce the very highest creations through your own creative efforts, but it is also necessary to obtain that wisdom, or interior insight through which the proper selections may be made from those other sources that do invariably contribute to your fate.

Those creations of nature that we may find in our own environment, are filled with unlimited possibilities, whether they appear favorable or not. What they are to do to us depends upon what we decide to do with them.

We may take the elements of nature and convert them into high and constructive uses, or we may permit ourselves to remain in bondage to those elements. The bondage, however, is not produced by nature, but the way we relate ourselves to nature.

To master that part of fate that we receive from nature, the secret is to be in harmony with nature at all times, and under all conditions, and to try constantly to employ constructively every element in nature with which we may come in contact.

That part of fate that has been received from the race is called heredity, and is usually looked upon as a permanent factor in life; but there is no heredity that can not be changed.

Acquire the art of letting those things go that you do not want, and proceed to improve upon those that you do want.

Use undeveloped hereditary conditions as channels through which to reach the greater things you have in view. Back of every condition there is a power; that power can be developed, and when it is, the old, inferior condition disappears.

What is called the "world," with all its perversions and obstacles, is simply raw material, out of which the strong mind can build almost anything that he may desire. But the "world" must not be met in the belief that things as they are, are permanent and insurmountable; but as the builder meets his material.

Work in the idea that "he can who thinks he can;" develop interior insight so that you may know how to select the material you desire; and develop your mind into a strong mind by entering the attitude of self-supremacy.

We have the same mental power over circumstances and conditions as we have physical power over iron, lumber and coal.

Every event that transpires in daily life contains an opportunity; but we must have the insight to see it, and the power to employ it.

The creation of those individuals with whom we come in personal contact, constitute frequently a predominating factor in our destiny, because since we are more or less wedded to our associations, our mlnds accept impressions from such sources to a very great degree; but this interferes with original thinking, and consequently, with our own mastery of fate.

Therefore, that part of fate that we receive from friends, relatives and personal associations, must be carefully selected through insight and through the principle that "when we become better, we meet better people." Instead of being indiscriminately influenced by our friends, we should accept their mental gifts as we accept their hospitable repast— to be masticated, digested and assimilated by ourselves.

What to do with close relations that refuse to co-operate with us, is a great problem that becomes extremely simple when we decide to live our own life in such a way that no person's liberty or idea of liberty is disturbed.

Be a model character that does things;

and everybody will soon go with you to the superior life you have in view.

Give your best to everybody and the best will certainly come to you if you give the law the time required, and do not force changes by impatience and lack of faith. Change yourself, and all other desirable changes must positively follow.

EVERY factor in the fate of man responds to the life of man; and every element in the life of man is governed, directed, changed or modified by the thought of man. Therefore, as thought goes, so will the creative causes of fate go also. For this reason, if fate is to be improved, thought must move upward and onward; and since thought follows ideals, to him who would master his fate, ideals become indispensable.

But it is not only necessary to have ideals; it is also necessary to make real our ideals. This, however, seems difficult for the average person to do, because between the real and the ideal there appears to be a gulf that he does not know how to bridge.

Even many of the greatest philosophers in the world have failed to realize in a practical way what their finer perceptions had discovered; though this is not strange, because it is the prophetic faculty that sees the ideal, and the scientific faculty that makes the ideal real; and these two faculties are not always found in the same man.

The complete man, however, has both; and he who would master his fate must be complete.

By the prophetic faculty we do not mean the power to discern the future, because with the future we are not concerned; we are living in the eternal now and in the eternal now we shall always continue to live.

The prophetic faculty is the power to look back of things, within things and above things; thus discerning basic laws, fundamental principles and the unbounded possibilities that exist everywhere. It is seeing the ideal; and the ideal is not a mere mental picture, but the discovery of something higher, something better and something greater than what is actually realized now. The prophetic faculty discovers what can be done now if we choose to do it.

This faculty is developed through the constructive use of the imagination, the constant use of interior insight, and the practice of looking for the greater possibilities in everything with which we come in contact.

The mere discovery of the great is not sufficient; the ideal must be made real. It is not the dreaming of things, but the doing of things that produces a better fate and a larger destiny. But we must perceive the greater things before we can do the greater things; and to perceive the greater things is to have ideals.

To make real the ideal, the scientific

faculty is required; and this faculty develops through scientific thinking and through the practical application of every principle and law discovered.

To make real the ideal, the first essential is to remove from consciousness the gulf that seems to exist between present attainment and the greater possibilities. Refuse to think of this gulf, because to think of it is to impress the mind with the idea that the greater is beyond us. This impression will prevent mind from reaching the greater, and will also produce frequent states of despair. Such states not only weaken mind, but cause man to give himself up to the influence of environment.

A discouraged mind, submitting itself to environment, is impressed with failure, weakness, inferiority, and the tendency to go down grade; while the mind that is to master fate must go the other way.

To remove the seeming gulf from mind, turn attention not only upon the ideal you desire to reach, but try to see the ideal of yourself as well. By so doing you impress the ideal of yourself upon your mind; thoughts like the ideal self will be created, and your personal self becomes like the thoughts you think. Consequently, by a simple process, the personal self is made to improve constantly, daily becoming more and more like the ideal.

To realize constant personal advancement is to prevent all thoughts of discouragement, and also to enter the power of that law through which gain promotes gain, and much gathers more.

The law is that you begin to realize the ideal in your personal life when the personal self begins to grow into the likeness of the ideal. Therefore, to yearn for ideals while nothing is being done to make yourself more ideal, is to continue to keep yourself away from your ideal.

It is like that attracts like, and only those who are alike will be drawn into the same world; consequently, to live in the same world with your ideal, you must become like your ideal.

The ideal can not come down to you; ideals never move that way; but you can go up to your ideal, and that is the true way for you to move.

To make any part of the personal self ideal, place before the creative powers of mind the corresponding ideal of your true self; and it must be remembered that your true self is not something distinct from your ideal self, because the two are one.

The ideal of yourself is you; you are the ideal side of yourself; the actual or external side of yourself is only a partial expression of the ideal or true self.

The ideal side of man is the complete

side; and the complete side is you. You are not the incomplete side, because if you were there would be no source for anything in your being; not even the incomplete or external side would have a source, and consequently could not exist.

Incompleteness can not come from incompleteness, because an incompleteness is a partial effect of a complete cause. Incompleteness can come only from completeness; therefore, the fact that the personal self is incomplete proves that it comes from a self that is complete; and since you, yourself, can not be complete and incomplete at the same time, you, yourself, must be the complete self, while the personal self is but a partial expression of the completeness that exists in you.

When you see this clearly, you will know that you are already ideal; that is, complete, and in possession of unlimited possibilities; and when you *know* that you are ideal, you will *think* of yourself as ideal. You will impress the ideal, and the greater possibilities upon mind, and your thoughts will not only be ideal, but will contain the power of the greater possibilities. This power will be expressed in the personal self, because the power of every thought is expressed in the personal self; consequently, the personal self will become larger, greater and more perfect, constantly making real the ideal.

To realize your ideal it is not necessary to change your present environment, or to adopt some radical mode of living; nor is it necessary to be transported to some other sphere.

The ideals that you see are in your own path, directly before you, and will positively be reached through a forward movement. We can not see the ideals of another mind; therefore, the ideals that you see are in your own path, and can be reached by you. The secret is to move forward in your own life. Be yourself, and bring out all that exists in yourself, and you will gain both the power and the ability to reach what you have in view.

There will be no waiting time; and it is not necessary to become absolutely perfect to make real the ideal. The very moment you begin to develop the personal self into the likeness of the ideal self, the ideal life will begin to become real in the personal life; and the mind that impresses itself only with its own selected and superior impressions, will develop the personal self with the greatest rapidity.

To make real the ideal, the principle is to make everything in your life more and more like the ideal.

Ideal friendship brings ideal friends;

refinement in action, thought and speech brings refined people; greater ability brings greater results in the world of achievement; and better environments come when we develop the power to create the better. A beautiful mental life produces a beautiful physical existence; and by giving the best to the world, the best will surely return.

**F**ATE is created by the powers in man; therefore, in order to master fate, man. must acquire control over the creative forces in his being. And this is accomplished, not by trying to control these forces, but by changing their courses.

Every force in the system moves through the field of consciousness, and by training the will to act upon consciousness so as to open or close the channels of consciousness in any place, the different forces in the system can be directed wherever desired.

No force can be driven. We can not drive the force of electricity; but by providing suitable conductors, electricity will go wherever it is wanted, because we have the power to move the conductors about as we like.

The channels of consciousness, more correctly designated the tendencies of mind, are the conductors of the creative forces of the system; therefore, by regulating the tendencies of mind we may cause all, or any desired part of our creative power to accumulate at any time in any place of mind or body.

To regulate the tendencies of mind, the

will must act upon the finer or inner side of consciousness; and whatever the will wills to have done while acting upon the finer side, the same will be done.

To reach this finer side, mind must enter a perpetual refining process, and must establish this process in every part of the system. Create a strong desire to transform, refine and improve everything with which you come in contact, and the finer consciousness will develop steadily. This is the first essential.

The second essential is to properly meet the forces that come into your life, because every force that comes, comes to act; and how it is met will determine whether its action upon you will be favorable or not.

When you meet a force, you must do something with it, or it will do something with you; you must direct it, or it will pass through your system aimlessly and be lost. Or, if it is an undeveloped force, as most forces are, you will permit the formation of adverse conditions by permitting such a force to pass through your world unguided.

It is the nature of all forces to do things; they can not be idle; therefore, if you do not give them something definite to build, they will build aimlessly, or destroy ruthlessly.

We are constantly in the midst of powerful forces, and they are all at our command when we know how to command them; but they do not pass under our dominion until they enter our systems.

It is the forces that pass through our own systems that we can direct; and when these are properly directed, anything we desire to have done can be done; because an enormous amount of energy is generated in the average person, and hourly passes through the person.

When we learn to direct and constructively employ all those forces, it matters not whether we have highly developed parents or not; whether we have a good ancestry or not; whether we were born under favorable conditions or not; whether we have any talents and opportunities or not; we can make ourselves over absolutely; we can change and improve everything in ourselves and in our environments, and proceed in the creation and realization of a great and superior destiny.

When we place ourselves in a favorable attitude towards all the forces that enter the system, and learn how to direct those forces into favorable channels of construction, every force that passes through the system will become favorable to us, no matter where it comes from, nor how unfavorable it may be before it enters our *favorable world.*

The secret is to make your own system a transforming, refining and transmuting power. Establish in your system two predominating tendencies and desires—to refine everything and to construct superiority out of everything. And every force that enters your system will become a superior constructive power for you; and will build up your talents, promote your purpose, and change your fate as you wish it to be.

The whole world of power is ready to build for the man that is thoroughly permeated with the desire to become more and accomplish more; therefore, the man who lives constantly in the spirit of transformation will reach the highest goal he has in view.

Make no effort to control or influence any force within yourself, or outside of yourself. Simply control yourself to remain constantly in constructive touch with the finer vibrations of the world of force.

It is necessary to meet every force in the serene attitude, and to *feel* an interior oneness with the real life of all power. When you feel this deeper unity, every force will unite with you, work for you, and promote your purpose.

When the presence of a force is felt in the system, we should enter into mental touch with the inner, finer side of that force, and hold strongly in mind what we desire to accomplish. This will produce the tendency required, and the force will follow the new channel, to do what we desire to have done.

To develop this finer and interior feeling, enter into constant sympathy with the inner life of everything, and be always in poise. Employ the finer senses of perception, discernment and deep feeling as frequently as possible, and try every day to *feel through* your entire system.

Concentrate several times daily upon the higher vibrations that are back of, within and above every atom in your being; and whenever you use the will, turn attention upon the soul or real *substance* of things.

HE creative forces that are generated in man, and the cosmic forces that work through man are fundamental causes of fate; therefore, if man would master his fate, he must consciously direct these so that the creations may be what he desires. When he fails to do this, the creative forces will be directed or influenced by suggestions from external conditions and environments; and this is what takes place in the life of the average person; therefore, his fate is so uncertain, so mixed and so unlike his secret ideal.

The methods presented in the previous chapter will enable any one to get into that state of consciousness where the forces of the system can be turned in any direction; but after a power is under our control, we want to use it wisely, and to the very best advantage.

Good judgment, reason, understanding, and a brilliant intellect will serve this purpose to a degree; but to make the very best use of every power, under every circumstance, another faculty is required. The necessary faculty is interior insight; or the power to discern the causes, principles and laws that lie beneath the surface. It is that sense that all possess to a degree, that feels and knows how things are going, and how they ought to go; and may therefore be called the inside secret of all success, of all great attainments and achievements.

It is through this faculty that man does the right thing at the right time, with or without the aid of external evidence.

The great minds who have taken advantage of exceptional opportunities at the psychological moment, have been prompted to do so by this very faculty; and what is usually termed extraordinary good fortune is but the result of actions that interior insight was instrumental in producing.

No one has ever reached the pinnacle of attainment and achievement without this faculty, and no one ever will. In the absence of interior insight, the greater part of the best ability would be misdirected, and most of the powers of the system would be lost.

Interior insight is not a faculty that has to be acquired; everybody has it to a considerable degree; it is only necessary that it be further developed and consciously employed. And as it deals directly with the finer forces of life, discerning the nature, the present movements and the latent possibilities of those forces, it is in connection with the world of those forces that the faculty must be exercised for greater efficiency.

To bring this faculty into full expression so it may be employed with accuracy in any field desired, the first essential is to exercise interior insight at every possible opportunity. Not that its verdict should be invariably accepted; but its verdict should always be sought. It will be profitable to do this even in minute and unimportant daily affairs, because it is by discerning the law of action in small things, that we gain the power to discern the same law in greater things.

When this faculty is developed, we shall no longer judge according to appearances, and be misled; but we shall judge according to the real facts that are at the foundation of things; and since it is the underlying causes that must be dealt with in the mastery of fate, interior insight becomes indispensable.

Whenever you are in the midst of changes, or have anything to decide, *expect* to discern the proper course, and decide correctly through the action of interior insight. And have perfect faith in the power of this faculty at all times. This will not only strengthen the faculty, but will in most instances produce the decision desired.

When conflicting ideas come at such times, enter into a deep, serene state of mind, forgetting the various ideas received, and desiring with the whole of life to discern what you wish to know. Remain in this attitude for days if necessary, or until you receive only one leading decision on the subject. You will get it, and the strong, prolonged effort will have developed your interior insight to a remarkable degree.

To determine the reliability of an idea received through insight, test it with reason, from every point of view; and if it continues to remain a predominant conviction, it is the truth of which you are in search.

While expecting information through this faculty, mind should be kept as quiet and as elevated in thought as possible. All sentimental or emotional feelings should be avoided, and the imagination must be perfectly still.

The upward look of mind, devoid of restless yearning, but fully serene and responsive, is the true attitude.

Expect to receive the desired information from the superior wisdom of your higher mentality, and know that there positively is such a wisdom.

While expecting this superior wisdom to unfold what you desire to know, be positive to your environment and to everything in the without. Do not permit the senses to suggest anything on the subject. But be responsive to your interior life; that is, feel in the within that your mind is open to the real wisdom from the within.

Never doubt the existence of the superior wisdom within. This will close the mind to that wisdom. You know that there is such a wisdom; you have evidence to prove it every day; and the more faith you have in its reality, the more perfectly will your mind respond to its unfoldment.

Another essential to the full expression of interior insight is to refine the physical brain so that the finer mental actions may produce perceptible impressions. This is accomplished by awakening the finer forces of the system, and directing those forces through a deep, serene concentration, upon every part of the brain. This exercise should be taken for a few minutes, several times a day; and the more highly refined you feel throughout the system at the time, the greater the results.

In the use of interior insight, reason and objective understanding should not be ignored, because the best results are secured when the exterior and interior aspects of judgment are developed simultaneously and used together at all times. In this way the mind acquires the power to discern the internal causes on the one hand, and on the other, understands how to adapt the present movements of those causes to present exterior conditions. This brings the ideal and the practical into united action at every turn, which is absolutely necessary.

While exercising the faculty of interior insight, the predominant effort should be to *see through* things; because the predominant desire, if continued, is always realized.

THE place that each individual is to occupy in the world is determined principally by character and ability; there are other factors, all of which have been mentioned, but these two predominate.

When character is absent, the powers of mind or body will be turned into wrong channels, because nothing in the being of man can go right unless it passes through the life of character.

When ability is absent, man becomes a negative personality, incapable of creating a single course of individual action, and is consequently influenced and controlled by everything with which he comes in contact.

The reason why so many beautiful characters are found in undesirable environments is because they lack positive creative ability.

It is ability that supplies the power to do things; and it is character that directs the power so that the things done will be worthy and true.

By character, however, we do not mean simply a state of being good in the ordinary sense of that term; nor is it a mere attitude of mind that holds preference for the right.

Character is an established quality of being, based upon the principle of absolute right. It is a living power with divine. consciousness as its source; it is a life that is right, and that thrills every atom in being with the force of justice, righteousness and truth.

Character is a permanent attainment; it can not be shaken; it can not, under any consideration, be influenced from without; but it can at all times be unfolded from within.

That character should be necessary in the mastery of fate, is evident when we realize that all the creative powers of man must express themselves through the principle of the absolutely right, if they are to create a better and a greater destiny; because it is through character alone that the right expression of any force or any talent can take place.

Develop ability, and develop character, and you have the foundation for any fate you may desire to create. You have that something that wins every time, regardless of seeming exceptions.

With character and ability combined, no one can fail; and with a high development of these two, any one can attain, not only great things, but the very greatest of all things.

To promote the highest development and the most thorough use of character and ability, faith becomes indispensable.

Faith awakens everything within us that is superior, and brings out the best that is within. Faith unites man with the Infinite; and no one can accomplish the great things in life unless he works constantly in oneness with the Infinite. No mind can do much without the Supreme; and no one can do his best in any sphere of action unless he lives so near to the Supreme that the divine presence is consciously felt at all times.

We *are* helped by a higher power, and we can receive far greater assistance and far superior assistance from this same source when our faith is high and strong.

A highly developed mind may accomplish much without faith, but with faith that same mind can accomplish a great deal more; and the same is true of every mind in every stage of development. Faith increases the power, the capacity and the efficiency of everything and everybody.

One of the greatest essentials in the mastery of fate is to have a high goal, a definite goal, and to keep the eye single upon this goal. And there is nothing that causes the mind to aim as high as faith. Faith goes out upon the boundlessness of all things; it passes by the borderland and

93

proves there is no borderland. It demonstrates conclusively that all things are possible, and that there is no end to the path of attainment; and what is more, it demonstrates that this path to greater and greater attainment is substantial and sound all the way. There is no seeming void; all is solid rock; therefore, it is perfectly safe to go out anywhere into the universal. In the eyes of faith, there is no gulf between the small and the great; from the smaller to the greater there is a path of smooth and solid rock, and any one may safely reach the greater by simply pressing on.

To master fate, the mind must be determined to reach the highest goal in view, and should realize that the goal can be reached—that it is being reached. And there is nothing that makes the mind more determined to reach the heights than a strong, living faith.

Faith sees the heights; faith knows they are there, and can be reached. Therefore, to a mind that would create a grander fate, nothing is more valuable than faith.

To attain faith we must understand that it is not blind belief; it is not belief at all.

Faith is a live conviction, illumined knowledge received at first hand through the awakening of that power within that sees, knows and understands the spirit of things.

Consequently, faith not only awakens higher and mightier powers, and illumines the mind with light, wisdom and truth of incalculable value, but it also brings mind into perfect touch with those laws and principles that lie at the very foundation of all life, all attainment, all achievement, and all change; and it is these laws that mind must employ if fate is to be mastered, and a greater destiny created.

To attain faith, have faith; have faith in the Supreme; have faith in man; have faith in yourself; have faith in everything in the universe; and above all, have faith in faith.

Last, but not least, the man who would master his fate must do things in love. A tangible fate is the result of tangible deeds; but no tangible deed can contribute to a better fate unless is it the product of love.

Desire to do things with a desire that sets every fibre in being aflame; love everything that is being done, with a love that is the living power of the soul itself; and give yourself, your largest self, your whole self to your life and your work. And what you give that will be your fate.

Printed in the United States
216001BV00001B/20/A